BOWLING 300

Top Pros Share Their Secrets to Rolling the Perfect Game

DAN HERBST

CB
CONTEMPORARY
BOOKS
CHICAGO

Library of Congress Cataloging-in-Publication Data

Herbst, Dan.
    Bowling 300 : top pros share their secrets to rolling the
perfect game / Dan Herbst.
       p.   cm.
    Includes index.
    ISBN 0-8092-3823-3
    1. Bowling.   I. Title.   II. Title: Bowling three hundred.
GV903.H44   1993
794.6—dc20   93-11327
                                        CIP

10   9   8   7   6   5   4   3   2   1

CONTENTS

1

INTRODUCTION

There is nothing quite as dramatic in sports as when an athlete's skill and will are tested in one climactic moment. In baseball, it's a three-and-two pitch with the bases loaded. On a gridiron, it's when a field-goal kicker attempts to split the uprights with a game on the line. And in bowling, it's when 60 feet and 10 pins are all that separate the player from achieving a 300 game.

Perfection. It's personified by having the ability to think like Albert Einstein, look like Bo Derek, sound like James Earl Jones, and behave like Mother Teresa of Calcutta. Needless to say, it's a lofty ambition to which few of us pretend to strive and fewer still can ever hope to achieve.

Except in bowling.

The sheer thrill of achieving perfection—albeit for only one dozen deliveries—will be felt by about 15,000 people this year. Perhaps you will be one of those who, for one marvelous game, rise to produce a score that even the world's greatest player can never supersede.

There was a time when shooting a 300 was reserved

for the gifted few. Nobody could achieve that feat without a combination of tremendous talent and a commensurate amount of good luck.

During the 1963–64 season, more than 4.6 million league bowlers combined for a mere 829 perfect games. The odds on rolling a 300 at that time were less than one in a half million.

But with modernization, the chances of realizing the most recognized form of tenpin immortality have increased dramatically. Livelier pins, powerful urethane balls, and the overall improved athleticism of the contemporary adult combined to produce 14,192 perfect games in 1990–91 despite there being nearly one-third fewer bowlers than a generation ago. If you were to roll 20,595 games, say the odds, you figure to produce one contest featuring 12-out-of-12 strikes.

And that doesn't take into account all of the perfect games that didn't receive official American Bowling Congress sanction because they were rolled during nonleague play or because of a lane-conditioner infraction.

Kegling perfection comes in many packages. PBA superstar Pete Weber was only 12 when he rolled his first 300, while Hall of Fame member Helen Duval was 65 when she became the oldest woman to match Weber's score.

For several years, pros Bob Learn, Jr., and Jim Johnson, Jr., have been locked in a duel for producing the most sanctioned 300 games. As of this book's publication, Learn holds a 42–36 edge. A newcomer to the hunt is Cincinnati amateur Mike Whalin. He's turned the trick 37 times.

As impressive as these credentials are, I believe that the four coauthors of this work are qualified to offer the best advice on how you can join the 300 club.

Mark Baker has rolled so many perfect games that he admits to having lost count. The best guess is that, including those rolled in practice, he has long since eclipsed 50 such efforts.

Although he's lost count, Baker is well into his second half-century of 300s. (Photo by Steve Spatafore)

Walter Ray Williams has achieved perfection, and stardom, in two sports. The former PBA Player of the Year is a five-time world champion in pitching horseshoes. Williams was among a select few stars invited to visit the White House by then-President George Bush to toss shoes.

Marc McDowell, one of the rising young stars of the PBA Tour, combines great skill and intellect. The youngest

McDowell is a former collegiate star. (Photo by Steve Spatafore)

man (at age 28) to ever serve as PBA president, McDowell was honored as the pro circuit's top rookie in 1986 after a stellar collegiate bowling career at West Texas State University.

Of all the 300s ever rolled, none was more lucrative or dramatic than that produced by Bob Benoit. With a national television audience of several million viewers as witnesses, the Oklahoma native pocketed $162,550 for being invincible in his championship-round debut during the 1988 Quaker State Open. Benoit defeated all-time great Mark Roth, 300–255.

Baker, Williams, McDowell, and Benoit are all noteworthy for excelling on the PBA Tour for a long period of time, for being among the most articulate of their peers, and for their ability to string strikes. On the pages ahead, they offer scores of invaluable pointers on how you can achieve one of the most thrilling accomplishments in sports.

A glance at their credentials reveals that these men are very good at their occupations.

Mark Baker rolled his first perfecto on November 4, 1977, in the Greater Los Angeles Junior All-Star League, a traveling league that brings together the finest prospects from Southern California. The competition on that afternoon was at Arcadia's Bowling Square.

Although only 16, Baker was already physically impressive. By his junior year at Garden Grove High School, he stood 6'2" with a solid frame.

In but a few weeks, he would begin another basketball season for the Argonauts of coach Gene Campbell. As good as he was on the lanes, many thought that he was even more gifted on a court. Baker, a pragmatist who understands something about odds, was always realistic about which avenue provided the better chance at stardom. As he's fond of saying, "You don't find very many 6'4" power forwards in the NBA."

Scholastic hoops, however, has plenty of room for such types. Baker netted approximately 1,000 points in two-and-a-half seasons of varsity competition. Baker averaged 27 a game as a senior while earning All-American recognition.

As a boyhood buddy of future baseball standout Lenny Dykstra, Baker was forever competing against top athletes at a variety of sports. Those experiences helped him to develop extremely strong legs, which are a vital prerequisite to success in today's power-oriented game.

Baker made his PBA debut as a teenager in 1980. Two years later he toured full-time. In 1984 he established himself as one of his sport's best performers, winning his first national title, the Miller High Life Classic at Don Carter's Kendall Lanes in Miami.

Baker was seeded third entering the title round after having averaged 222.7 during the 42-game qualifying segment of the tournament.

In front of a capacity crowd and a national television audience, Baker destroyed veteran Rick Sajek, 268–206. He then eliminated Joe Salvemini, 194–180, to earn a title-game shot. The championship-game matchup featured two generations of power players. The arsenal of the far more experienced pro featured such a distinctive strike ball that he had long since been dubbed "Hookin' " Bob Handley.

On this day, however, it was the upstart whose pin-shattering prowess proved supreme. Baker claimed the $27,000 top prize by scoring a 221–183 upset victory.

Baker finished the year 10th on the PBA earnings list. That season began a streak of consistency that few pros have surpassed. In both 1985 and 1986, Baker was sixth on the PBA money list. He followed that by finishing 25th (1987), 19th (1988), 22nd (1989), and 18th (1990).

During that period, his official winnings ranged from a low of $61,777 (in 1987) up to $90,925 (in 1985).

Baker's titles include the 1986 King Louie Open, the

1987 Kessler Open, and the 1990 Oregon Open. He may be best remembered for having won what was arguably the most exciting televised match when he defeated Dave Ferraro, 279–278, in the 1985 Austin Open.

A back injury sidelined Baker for 1991 and all but the last few weeks of 1992. After extensive rehabilitation, he returned to a Tour in which rapid advancements in equipment and ball-drilling techniques made him feel "like a rookie again" at age 31.

For all of Baker's accomplishments, the first question that strangers ask upon learning his profession is whether he has ever rolled a perfect game. An incredulous stare usually results when Baker answers that he's produced "about 40" such games in competition. Since most PBA tournaments aren't sanctioned by the American Bowling Congress, Baker's name isn't on the ABC's official list of high rollers.

The specifics of most of his 300s have been forgotten. Aside from Baker's first such effort, the most memorable was when he produced his 13th PBA Tour perfect game. Upon a pro's first such score, he is presented with a distinguished-looking ring that has cavities for one dozen diamond chips. With each successive 300, a chip is awarded until the ring reaches its capacity.

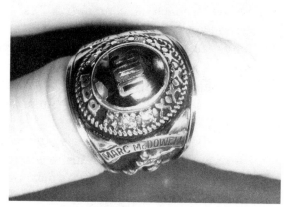

The PBA's 300 ring (McDowell version). (Photo by Steve Spatafore)

Baker's perfect game during the 1986 Budweiser Touring Players Championship in Taylor, Michigan, completed one of the more handsome pieces of jewelry in professional sports.

According to Baker, except when it's done in a televised title round, most pros don't consider rolling a 300 to be "that big a deal." Fans, however, view it differently. As the drama builds, the crowd grows behind that pair of lanes. By the final frame, most of the paying customers have crammed together. The center's normal noise level abates to an eerie silence similar to the calm before a tornado.

Those watching Baker are rarely disappointed. Once that 11th strike has been collected, number 12 is almost a foregone conclusion. For all of the 300s that he's rolled, Baker estimates that he's only shot "seven or eight" games of 298 or 299.

Perhaps that traces back to the confidence he gained that day in Arcadia. Being in a new situation didn't cause any loss in composure. Baker recalls taking very little time between shots based on the premise that progressing faster allowed less time to become nervous.

Through the years, Baker has come to view the 12th strike as far easier than its predecessors. For one thing, by that time his confidence level has grown. After all, one doesn't produce 11 consecutive "Xs" without executing several outstanding shots and, on the less-than-perfect deliveries, discovering that the pin gods are temporarily granting a comfortable margin for error.

"The more strikes that I string the easier it becomes because I know that I have got a great shot on that pair" of lanes, Baker explains.

To Baker, the 10th strike is often the most challenging. He freely concedes that during his formative years, he wasn't ranked among bowling's most polished spare shooters. He often settled for a score in the 260s after failing to fill the final frame.

Baker has always felt that once he gets the 10th strike, the guarantee of rolling a score in the high 280s removes a significant amount of pressure. By the end of his junior career, Baker had notched three more 300s. Within a year of joining adult leagues at age 18, he added an additional "five or six" perfect games.

Walter Ray Williams is equally adept at getting ringers as he is at avoiding a ringing 10 pin. He became the premier performer of 1986 by winning the True Value Open, the Fair Lanes Open, and the Hammer Open.

Williams's consistency is money ($100,000+ a year) in the bank. (Photo by Steve Spatafore)

His $145,550 paced the Tour by a wide margin. It marked the first of five times in his career, including four consecutive years, in which Williams reached the six-figure plateau. In the history of the PBA, only Marshall Holman (1983-1988) and Mark Roth (1977-1981) have bettered Williams's consecutive-year $100,000+ streak, while Brian Voss (1987-1990) and Amleto Monacelli (1988-1992) have equaled it.

Whereas Baker relies on power to strike, Williams counters with uncanny accuracy. His nickname of "Deadeye" is equally applicable with a horseshoe or a bowling ball in his hand. Williams is one of a handful of pros who have rolled 20 or more perfect games in PBA competition.

To become successful, a bowler must have at least one spot on the lane where he or she can be dominant.

Of course, it helps that as a pro he bowls 2,000 games a year. The typical amateur player, in contrast, can expect to roll about 100 games for every league in which he or she participates.

Williams would bowl even more except that he has another arena in which to compete. After being a three-time junior world champion in horseshoes, he captured that sport's ultimate tournament in the men's division in 1978, 1980, 1981, 1985, and 1991. Although there have been fewer than 100 perfect games in the history of that sport, Williams has achieved a record of 10 such efforts, including the only ones shot back-to-back.

His first 300 came in the fall of 1979 as a substitute in a scratch league. His success proved the adage of "third time lucky" given that the first two such attempts had seen him finish with scores of 298 (thanks to a nose hit that left the 4-6 split on his final shot) and a very unlucky 299 (a stubborn 7 pin marred a seemingly flawless delivery).

He proved the twin adage that "good things happen in

threes" during the 1992 Tums Classic in the Hartford suburb of Windsor Locks, Connecticut. Williams's three perfect games during that event tied a PBA record.

It was during match play on April 16 that Williams rolled two perfect games while averaging 250.8 during his eight matches. His first 300 victim was Dave Ferraro. Four games later he did it again, this time against Ray Edwards. Williams scored early against Edwards with a Brooklyn strike. The next time on that lane, he made the proper adjustment, moving his feet two boards to the left, and was in the pocket thereafter.

A big part of Williams's success in that event was being able to play his favorite shot (more on that in Chapter 4). To become successful, a bowler must have at least one spot on the lane where he or she can be dominant. The key to being a star as a pro is to be able to compete when the lanes aren't to one's personal liking. Williams, like his three coauthors, belongs to both enviable categories.

His blistering 242.6 average during the qualifying segment of the 1992 Tums Classic was nearly nine pins better than that of his nearest rival that week. His pinfall of 10,188 was the most by any player during a 42-game format of a 1992 PBA Winter Tour event.

This was not the first time he'd been so dominant. Williams bested Tom Baker's 10-year-old PBA record during the 1991 Beaumont PBA Doubles Classic for both 6 games (1615 pins/269.2 average) and 12 games (3052/254.3). Included in that was one perfect game.

As of press time, Williams has registered 27 300s while participating in PBA tournaments.

His most dramatic attempt at achieving perfection fell one pin and $100,000 short. That's the bonanza that he would have received from True Value Hardware had it not been for a stubborn 10 pin on his final shot of the opening game in the title round of the Leisure's Long Island Open.

His 299–245 win over Robert Lawrence just missed making Williams the sixth PBA competitor in more than 30 years and 6,000 games to roll a 300 on national television.

When asked on the air about what went wrong with his 12th delivery, Deadeye deadpanned, "There's one too many pins in that rack!"

McDowell teamed with Hall of Famer Dick Weber to win the Senior/Touring Pro Doubles Championship. (Photo courtesy of the PBA)

Like Baker and Williams, Marc McDowell is a multiple-sport star. Before transferring to West Texas State, he was a substitute placekicker for the Badgers of his hometown University of Wisconsin-Madison. While at Monona Grove High School, he had booted a 43-yard field goal. He once made three straight 55-yarders in practice.

Being able to succeed as a placekicker requires some of the same qualities one needs to be a top bowler: powerful legs and the ability to execute a skill under tremendous pressure.

McDowell won $51,285 in his first year as a pro bowler, a PBA rookie record that still stands. His break-through year came in 1989, when he claimed his first two pro titles. In May, McDowell captured the Fresno Open the hard way by winning three title-round games. Included were conquests of two surefire future Hall of Fame members. McDowell edged Williams, 218–209, and Monacelli, 249–188, before ousting fellow Wisconsin product Tony Marrese, 234–196. Less than three months later, he and the great Dick Weber won the Senior/Touring Pro Doubles Championship in Buffalo.

McDowell epitomizes the new generation of pro bowlers who arrive on the PBA Tour after excelling in collegiate programs. It was for the Buffaloes of West Texas State that McDowell produced his first perfect game in 1982.

The "Bowling Buffs" were in a tournament at Kansas State facing their archrivals from Wichita State. At that time, the two schools were dominant forces in college bowling. Their battles were always memorable.

The two programs have each produced several pros. Among the West Texas State alumni are McDowell, Mike Miller, Jack Jurek, Nathan Terry, and Mike Scroggins. In his tenure at Wichita State, Coach Gordon Vadakin has helped to develop the skills of Mike Jasnau as well as two PBA Rookies of the Year, Rick Steelsmith (1988) and Brad Kiszewski (1990).

McDowell's first 300 game is all the more impressive because he rolled it in a campus student center. McDowell diplomatically notes that most such facilities exist to provide recreation, so it's rare when the quality of the lane maintenance produces an environment that's conducive to high scoring.

In more direct terms, most such places are dungeons in which one almost expects to see Mario and Luigi hopping by looking for the princess. That McDowell's 300 was only the "second or third" such score in that building's annals is evidence enough of what he had to overcome that day.

"The conditions were fairly tough," McDowell admits. He also concedes that, like most of the rest of us, he was struck by a severe case of nerves as that game progressed.

Peer pressure was part of the equation. When you are the only member of one of the nation's premier teams without a 300 to your name, there is a certain amount of kidding at your expense. Moreover, McDowell's several previous flirtations with perfection had all ended without satisfaction.

McDowell recalls: "I was so nervous and I wanted it so badly that I couldn't let go of the ball. It was a high nose hit on the Brooklyn side, but somehow all of the pins collapsed. I just bent over and whispered to myself, 'Thank you, God.' I knew I hadn't deserved to strike."

Since that time, the 300s have come with relative frequency. Nevertheless, it took him nearly three years on the pro Tour before he shot his first perfect game in a PBA event. It occurred during the Pro-Am segment of the $500,000 Seagram Coolers United States Open in Atlantic City, New Jersey, in 1988. At press time, his career total is 16 perfect games, 10 of which occurred during PBA events.

McDowell's best year was 1992, when he became only the 17th pro bowler to pocket more than $150,000 in a single year. As the Tour's leading money winner, McDowell spent that campaign locked in a battle for Bowler of the Year honors with Dave Ferraro. McDowell prevailed.

His shining moment came when he captured the sport's most coveted crown by winning the Firestone Tournament of Champions. The chapter he wrote in that annual event, whose 52-player field is limited to those who have won PBA titles, represents what remains as probably the most dramatic title round in the Tour's history.

Danny Wiseman was McDowell's opponent in the

semifinal game. Wiseman had vowed to win the tournament for his father, who was dying of cancer. With Albert Wiseman watching from the stands, McDowell scored a 248–235 victory.

Afterward, both McDowell and the younger Wiseman fought back tears as they hugged Albert. The capacity crowd at Riviera Lanes in the Akron suburb of Fairlawn offered their consolation to the elder Wiseman with a standing ovation.

In an anticlimactic title game, McDowell began with five consecutive strikes before coasting to a 223–193 victory over veteran Don Genalo. For his labors, McDowell pocketed $60,000.

Popular veteran Dave Ferraro and McDowell dominated the Tour in 1992. (Photo by Dan Herbst)

That's almost small change compared to how Bob
Benoit enriched himself on January 23, 1988, at the Forum
Bowling Lanes in Grand Prairie, Texas. His payoff included the tournament's first prize of $27,000 and a
$100,000 perfect-game reward from True Value Hardware.
Assorted bonuses from manufacturers upped the ante to
staggering proportions for a player whose previous official
career earnings totaled a mere $41,032.

Although he had accumulated a 19–5 match-play record, thanks, in large part, to a weekly 222.5 mean, Benoit
was far from the favorite that afternoon. Among those
battling for the right to face him for the title were 33-time
champion Roth, another member of the sport's Hall of
Fame (Joe Berardi), and the man who would become that
year's Player of the Year (Brian Voss).

As for Benoit, he was thrilled to have gotten that far.
A few years before, he quit the Tour when it was clear that
he couldn't compete with the big boys on their own turf.
An extensive sabbatical to refine his game followed as he
"learned how to bowl all over again." Benoit gambled by
closing his successful auto-body shop in favor of a final
attempt at chasing his dream.

Except for covering the 4-pin spare in the third frame,
Roth matched Benoit strike-for-strike until the eighth
stanza. When the superstar blinked, the underdog took
full advantage.

Benoit thus joined Jack Biondolillo (1967 Firestone
Tournament of Champions), Johnny Guenther (1969 San
Jose Open), Jim Stefanich (1974 Midas Open), Pete McCor-
dic (1987 Greater Los Angeles Open), and Gene Stus (1992
Pacific Cal Bowl Senior Open) as the only men to roll a 300
in a PBA title round aired on national television.

Buoyed by that payday, Benoit finished 1988 behind
only Voss in official earnings with $171,695. Proving he
wasn't a flash in the pan, Benoit placed 14th in the 1989

Benoit's televised 300 made PBA history.
(Photo courtesy of the PBA)

standings, was 32nd a year later, and his $116,965 was 8th in 1991.

He added two more trophies in 1991, and his title-round winning percentage (.769) based on a 10-3 record, was bettered only by Bowler of the Year David Ozio.

Benoit's recent exploits belie a less-than-auspicious beginning. His first perfect game was ample evidence that one can sometimes produce big numbers despite rolling an anemic strike ball. Before the 10th frame, his teammates were razzing him with insults such as, "Do you think you can get that sissy ball of yours to hit hard enough to carry the next three strikes?"

The 17-year-old bowler answered in the affirmative. It

was that game at Jupiter Bowl in Garland, Texas, that convinced Benoit he had potential. Until that point, Benoit's only booster was Cecil Pye, whose stepdaughter, Vicki, was dating Benoit. Pye worked with Benoit on improving his skills and his confidence. He was forever telling the youngster that he could become a good player. Says a grateful Benoit, "He really pushed me to better myself."

Words, however encouraging, only go so far. It took the deed of rolling a 300 to convince Benoit that Pye might be right. His first fling as a pro was distinguished only by clearly illustrating the areas of the game that Benoit needed to upgrade if he was to become successful. Benoit's recollections of his two-and-a-half-year overhaul toward a power game (found in the following chapter) provide several useful suggestions to anyone trying to follow in his footsteps.

While it's unlikely you will reap a financial windfall should you roll a 300, you will never forget the sheer thrill of the accomplishment.

Step one is believing in yourself. Even with all that he'd done to improve, Benoit acknowledges coming very close to backing out of the 1988 Quaker State Open at the 11th hour.

"I was scared," he admits. "A lot of people told me when I left Topeka that I was crazy to try again. Nobody believed in me except Cecil Pye and myself." Several times during his drive to the tournament site in Dallas, he came close to turning around. "Something," he says, "kept me going."

His goal was simply to be among the 53 pros in the 160-man field to earn a paycheck. Never in his wildest dreams did he envision himself winning, much less making history in the process. He gained some confidence when he struck out in the 10th frame to defeat Roth in the position-round game on Friday night.

Prior to Saturday's TV finals, veteran star Ozio said something that boosted Benoit's ego. "He told me that I had bowled so well all week that the tournament was mine," Benoit recalls.

Benoit was so focused before rolling the final few shots that he couldn't even remember the size of the bonanza that awaited the author of a 300 game. When the last pin fell, Benoit says, he "lost all contact with earth."

Roth told him it was the greatest bowling performance under pressure that he'd witnessed. It was certainly the most lucrative.

While it's unlikely you will reap a financial windfall should you roll a 300, you will never forget the sheer thrill of the accomplishment. On the pages ahead, the four pros and I will do our best to help you to realize that fantasy.

Dan Herbst

2

THE DELIVERY

Many athletic endeavors involve a trade-off between power and accuracy. The more of one that you strive for, the less of the other you will have. To find a balance is vital. All the power in the world does you no good if your shot misses the pocket. Being accurate isn't worth much if you can't carry.

Most players can be classified as either power- or accuracy-oriented. But to be successful requires compromise. Two-time Player of the Year Amleto Monacelli, triple-crown winner Pete Weber, and Bob Benoit are noted for their power. Although each has a devastating strike ball, none of them "revs it up" as much as do the game's ultracrankers.

Having power gives them an edge on the opposition. It allows them to carry those half-hits and, in bowling lingo, "opens up the lane." That means that they can miss their target by a few inches and either hit the pocket or come sufficiently close so as to still strike (or get a nine count on shots on which others would be faced with a difficult multiple-pin leave).

*Monacelli combines
power and accuracy.
(Photo courtesy
of the PBA)*

What makes Benoit, Weber, and Monacelli special is that their deliveries are under control. They aren't so power-happy that they lack consistency in hitting the pocket. Each could add several revs to his shots if he so chose, but they realize that the slight gain in carry and area created would be more than offset by the greater number of difficult spares and splits they could leave due to being less accurate.

There are also pros whose trademark is their pinpoint control. Those who rely primarily on a traditional style are more successful if, like David Ozio and Brian Voss, their ball drives through the pins after hitting the pocket. There are others who might be better than Ozio or Voss at hitting a target but who lack the requisite strong release to exploit the accuracy.

To most fans, it may seem that Monacelli personifies power while Voss epitomizes accuracy. To those in the know, the greatness of both comes from being fantastic in one category and above average in the other.

The success of both types of players proves that there is more than one way to skin the proverbial cat. It would be difficult to find a quartet of bowlers who can out-strike Baker, McDowell, Benoit, and Williams. Yet, their styles cover bowling's entire spectrum.

Although the ways that they get to the line are very different, both Baker and Benoit certainly belong in the power-oriented category. Benoit achieves his power by using less speed with more ball revolutions. Baker, who physically towers over Benoit, throws his shots much faster.

Today's pros differ from players of previous generations. The most conventional contemporary style will only find success if it's married with a strong release. The trend in the modern game is unmistakable; power, not accuracy, is more treasured today.

There can be little doubt that the introduction of urethane balls and the influence of all-time greats Mark Roth and Marshall Holman have combined to change bowling dramatically. Roth, especially, broke all of the style rules with his fast feet, considerable ball speed, big hook, and power. He was as different from what came before him as Michael Jordan's dunks are from the old hoop days of set shots and chest passes.

Roth's exciting style caught the imagination of the young bowlers of the 1970s and 1980s. Talk to today's stars, and it's amazing the number who name him as their boyhood hero.

Roth's influence became even more pronounced when the introduction of urethane balls in the early 1980s turned the tide in favor of players who crank it up. His 221.662

Tour average in 1979 is a record that wasn't seriously challenged for 14 years. The closest that anyone had come to erasing Roth's mark was Dave Ferraro's 219.702 in 1992. Had Ferraro knocked over an additional 2,000 pins, he still wouldn't have replaced Roth in the record book.

As in everything, success begets emulation. So alluring was the Roth style that the "right" way to bowl changed forever. Old theories were revised.

Prior to Roth, conventional thinking was that a delivery must be smooth, with one's hips and shoulders parallel to the foul line and all movements being perpendicular to it. The armswing was supposed to be as straight as Pat Boone, with the ball gently glided onto the lane.

Roth might be the most influential performer in his sport's history. (Photo courtesy of the PBA)

Accuracy, not power, was the primary contributing factor to becoming a great player.

To be sure, the traditional wisdom retains much merit, especially for those who only bowl one or two times a week. The fewer games you roll, the more that having a simple style will make it easier for you to duplicate your movements. That, in turn, will make you more consistent.

As for the more popular current style, its best recommendation is that you won't have to be nearly as exacting to strike consistently because the added power will allow you to get an "X" on many less-than-perfect deliveries.

When the power-only types are hot, they are virtually unbeatable. However, the feast-or-famine nature of this style isn't conducive to making a good living as a Touring pro or to helping a team do well in league play. The bowler who obtains a 550 series by rolling 190–175–185 helps the team in two of three games (by beating one's average) and doesn't hurt teammates with a horrible game. The one who rolls 145–255–150 can seemingly win a game single-handedly but is also responsible for putting his or her side in a big hole two out of every three games.

Just like in the tale of the tortoise and the hare, being steady often wins the race. Better yet, be steady at a good scoring pace.

What follows is a look at the "traditional" style, followed by pointers on maximizing power. Through lots of practice and experimentation, you can combine the principles of each so as to become a player who has sufficient quantities of both accuracy and power to get the job done.

BOWLING "BY THE BOOK"

The fundamental components of the conventional style are:

1. A pendulum armswing that rises above the waist but not above the shoulders at the height of the backswing.

Note Williams's steady head, good timing, and great leverage at the line. (Photo by Steve Spatafore)

2. Coordination between the armswing and footwork so that your slide concludes as you release your shot (known as being "in time").
3. Keeping your head steady, with your eyes riveted on your target throughout the delivery.
4. A smooth exit from the ball, rolling the shot onto the lane.
5. At conclusion, following through toward your target.
6. Smooth movements, from start to finish, directed toward the target.

An analysis of these follows.

A slightly unorthodox aspect of McDowell's delivery sees his hips jut to the left to make room for his outside-in armswing. (Photo by Steve Spatafore)

The Armswing

Conventional wisdom calls for allowing the ball to swing your arm and not the other way around. Try to picture a pendulum in which a string (represented by your arm) is propelled by the momentum of a heavy object (the ball). Understanding this principle is central to an "ideal" swing.

If it's done correctly, your arm will naturally move in a straight line. Throughout your delivery, the plane of the swing allows the ball to be as near to your body as feasible without striking against your leg. Ideally, gravity, **not** your muscles, will provide most of the force for the delivery.

The human physique makes it impossible to totally disengage all of your muscles. As Williams notes, the arm pivots around one's shoulder socket so that the concept of a pendulum is slightly modified due to an inherent amount of moderate physical restraint.

The address position of the stylist is holding the ball between chest and waist height. The ball's center is in line with the shoulder of your bowling arm. This allows you to execute a pushaway that's on the same plane as your armswing.

Move the ball forward as if you were handing it to an imaginary person. Let gravity cause the ball to fall to begin the armswing.

Naturally, the higher you hold the ball in the address position and the higher you hand it forward during your pushaway, the greater the distance it must fall to reach the bottom of the swing. The greater that distance, the greater the potential energy that's created (from physics class we are reminded of the principle that bodies in motion tend to stay in motion while bodies at rest tend to stay at rest).

This makes for a higher backswing, which, in turn, enhances the gravitational pull to help to create a faster descent. Your ball is moving more rapidly, increasing the speed of your shot.

To decrease ball speed, hold the ball lower during your address and have a lower pushaway.

Does this mean that there is absolutely no muscle power involved? Hardly. While a 100 percent "unmuscled" swing is the ideal, it's not realistic. What is important is to limit the amount that your arm guides the ball. The less muscle power employed, the less chance that your swing will wander off line. The result: optimum accuracy even while performing under pressure.

Not every bowler's armswing travels in a straight line. Baker's wraps slightly behind his back so that it's slightly counterclockwise as it moves forward. While he thinks this helps to increase his hook, he recommends the so-called "outside-inside swing" only for those to whom it comes naturally.

Baker advises: "Do what feels the most comfortable. The one thing that you should avoid is changing your armswing in order to make an adjustment. That's one aspect of my delivery with which I would never tinker."

Timing

There are three possibilities regarding the relationship of your footwork to your armswing. They can coincide, which is known as being "in time." Alternatively, your footwork can conclude prior to the release of your shot ("late timing") or before you let go of the ball ("early timing").

Being "in time" was always the choice of the stylist. To do that consistently requires the coordination of the armswing and footwork throughout the delivery.

The great majority of bowlers use a five-step delivery. A handful prefer to go the four-step route, which is how Williams was taught to bowl. Any number of steps beyond four are used to help obtain more consistent timing. Many people prefer the added step because they find it more comfortable not to have to synchronize the start of their footwork with their pushaway.

The principles of both methods are similar. The biggest difference is that the five-step player takes one step before putting the ball into motion. It's usually a very short stride. As it ends, the pushaway begins so that the forward movement of the ball finishes at

The one thing that you should avoid is changing your armswing in order to make an adjustment.

the same time as does the player's second step. (The second step in a five-step delivery is the same as the first step for those using the four-step method.)

The ball is at the bottom of your armswing on the next stride and reaches the top of the backswing as you make your next-to-last step. As previously noted, the slide coincides (or just slightly precedes) the release.

Five-step players begin by moving the foot that's opposite from their bowling hand, while those using four steps begin with the foot that's on the same side. Most people seem to find that it's easier to obtain consistent timing using five steps. This is especially true for the "occasional" bowler (defined here as anyone who rolls 10 or fewer games in a typical week).

The chances are good that if you had formal coaching, you were initially taught the four-step method. Teaching pros tend to consider it a good primer because its concepts are simple to grasp and easier to execute initially. Sooner or later, the great majority of bowlers decide to add that fifth step.

Many of the Tour's smaller players use five (or more) steps. The higher the number of strides, the quicker one's feet tend to move, generating greater ball speed.

To modify early timing, slow down the ball movement

on your first step or make your pushaway go slightly upward. To correct lateness, put the ball in motion sooner during your delivery.

The Pushaway

In a good pushaway, you appear to hand the ball to an imaginary person. Extend your arm in front of you so that gravity, not your muscles, causes the ball to descend.

The accepted theory is that your elbow should be locked in a straight position (see pages 48 and 49 for Bob Benoit's exception to this rule).

A front view of Baker's pushaway. (Photo by Steve Spatafore)

While Don Carter's bent elbow won't work for everyone, it didn't stop him from being a six-time Bowler of the Year. (Photo courtesy of the PBA)

A bent elbow, while unorthodox, isn't necessarily wrong. The great careers of Earl Anthony and Don Carter are proof of that. Nevertheless, the bend definitely inhibits your ability to generate maximum ball speed and it can make your armswing more muscled.

A Shakespearean Twist: All's right that starts right (Williams's accuracy begins with a straight pushaway). (Photo by Steve Spatafore)

Footwork

Many coaches teach heel-to-toe footwork. On every step, the heel of your foot touches the lane first, with the toes landing later. Doing so helps to keep your weight back. You will remain more upright from your waist, with your knees doing the bending. The result is greater leverage at the point of release for added power.

Like most pros, Williams uses heel-to-toe footwork. (Photo by Steve Spatafore)

Your last (sliding) stride should be your longest. It should end with your toes pointed either straight ahead or slightly inward.

Ideally, your sliding foot should be perpendicular to the foul line during your release for maximum balance and leverage.

Your footwork should start with what is as much a shuffle movement as a step. Each succeeding stride should be longer and faster than the one before. This maintains a rhythm and creates momentum. There are players who don't follow this rule who do just fine. Some bowlers have a shuffle step in the middle of their deliveries. Players who would otherwise suffer from "fast feet" (the sliding foot arriving at the line far in advance of the ball) use the shuffle step as a mid-delivery correction.

The best way to determine your natural starting position is by walking to the foul line and facing the settee area. Four-step bowlers take four big strides and then a half step back (to allow for having a long slide). Five-step bowlers take five brisk steps and then add a half step. You have probably discovered the best distance from the foul line for your game during your address.

Leverage

In the ideal release position, the player bends from the knees, not from the waist. This allows you to deliver the ball onto the lane, not into it.

Stand fairly upright throughout your delivery. The knee of your sliding leg should be either directly underneath your shoulders or slightly ahead of them. Imagine the foul line extending upward to the ceiling. You want the knee of your sliding leg to be the same distance from that

A good knee bend at the line is a big plus for rolling a powerful strike ball. (Photo by Steve Spatafore)

line as your shoulders or slightly closer to it.

While a good knee bend is important, you don't want to overdo it. Bending your knee too low forces you to bend your elbow so that the ball doesn't hit the floor during your downswing. In the ideal release position, the bottom of the bowling ball is roughly six inches off the floor with your arm straight.

Release the ball within inches of the ankle of your sliding foot for maximum leverage. The greater the distance from ankle to the ball, the less power you'll have. In addition, you'll have a tendency to "circle" the ball in an attempt to pull it toward your target, which causes you to come around the side of the ball with your follow-through. This produces too much spin and not enough roll, which hinders carry.

The Release

One aspect of the game that really separates the exceptional from the mediocre player is the quality of the hand release. You need to develop an excellent release if you are to become a striking machine.

A common mistake of amateurs is to rotate the hand so that the thumb faces the floor during the release. This is known as "topping" a shot. This provides only a small portion of the side spin that's required for a strong hook. The result is often a weak hit, and it becomes almost impossible to take advantage of lane conditions by throwing a good hook shot.

Others "spin" their shots by coming completely around the ball. This technique is equally undesirable. Williams says that one of the greatest misconceptions that bowlers have is thinking that they must impart spin to their shots. The result, he notes, is that "they screw it like a top. That's not the way to release a shot."

Many pros keep their hands "locked" in the same position throughout the delivery until the release. In most cases, at the bottom of the armswing the thumb is between 1 and 2 o'clock on the ball (lefties are between 10 and 11 o'clock).

Make sure to conclude your shot with a straight follow-through. As you do so, reach out at your target and let your arm swing naturally toward the ceiling.

To get your ball to roll a little sooner, turn your thumb toward 10 or 11 o'clock (1 or 2 o'clock for a left-handed player). Lock into that position throughout, gripping the ball almost as if it were a suitcase. Your shot will roll sooner and hook less.

There are times when you will want more side turn so your ball will skid through the head area of the lane and finish with a sharper and more powerful break at the end. With 10 to 11 o'clock as your starting position, slightly rotate your hand counterclockwise (lefties clockwise). The twisting motion begins at the bottom of your swing, just before you release your shot.

As you let go, the thumb moves upward toward the noon position. The right-handed player's thumb rotates from 2 o'clock to 1 o'clock during the release to noon at the conclusion of the follow-through. The southpaw starts at 10, is at 11 at the release, and concludes at 12 o'clock. Make sure to come through the ball, never over it.

Wrist Positions

Another way of altering the amount that your shot hooks is by changing your wrist position. If you "cup" your wrist, the ball will hook earlier and a lot more. To delay and minimize hook, break your wrist backward. Keeping your wrist in a flattened (straight) position allows for a hook that falls between the two extremes.

While Benoit cups his wrist to maximize his hooking and carrying power, McDowell always has his in a natural (flat) position. (Photo by Steve Spatafore)

Lofting

If you are hitting the pocket but not carrying, rollout could be your problem. It occurs when your ball expends a great (and unnecessary) amount of energy getting through the head oil. By the time it reaches the pins, far too much of your shot's power is already expended. The pocket-entry angle of your hook is decreased or eliminated (in bowling lingo, your shot "flattened out"). When this happens, your ball is deflected by the headpin just as if you had thrown a straight shot.

Negating the heads is everyone's goal, but few bowlers are completely successful. Two of the best are Mark Roth and Dave Ferraro. Both loft their shots.

It isn't necessary to throw the ball halfway down the lane on the fly to beat the oil pattern. Just loft your shot so that it travels one to five feet past the foul line before landing on the lane. The "optimum distance," in Williams's opinion, "is two to three feet."

Benoit uses loft to get this shot through the head area. (Photo by Steve Spatafore)

Make sure that you release the ball as it's moving parallel to the floor. You want it to move outward. Never lose the ball on the downswing or toss it after your hand has moved upward.

The amount of desired loft varies with the lane condition. The drier the head area, the earlier your shot will hook. To avoid rollout and to obtain the desired skid-roll-hook pattern, utilize maximum loft. Very oily heads call for little or no loft.

On the PBA Tour, the heads are oily during morning blocks and drier in the evenings. Unless you are familiar with the maintenance schedule of the center where you are bowling, you will need to discover the lane condition as you compete.

Ball Speed

Contrary to popular misconception, speed does not equal power. A ball thrown too fast causes pins to fly over, not into, the back row. You want the front pins to stay low to the lane so they remain in play.

Shots rolled too slowly also hinder carry because they don't take advantage of the side walls to allow pins to ricochet back onto the deck. Slowness can also cause an overreaction to the lane's oil pattern.

To increase speed, stand farther back on the approach and hold the ball higher during the address. To slow down, hold the ball lower during the address. If you find yourself leaving a lot of corner pins, try throwing the ball a little slower.

So much for the "rules" governing how you should bowl. Each of our four pros has nuances and idiosyncrasies that defy conventional wisdom. By studying their styles, you can discover alternatives that you might wish to incorporate into your game. We'll begin with an analysis of McDowell's form.

THE McDOWELL STYLE

The leading money winner of 1992 says that you don't have to be infatuated with power to out-strike your opponent. Many league players should rethink their love affairs with the appeal of shattering pins.

Marc McDowell observes: "Most players are concerned with putting a lot of revs on the ball. They want to throw the strongest ball around. When I grew up, kids were emulating Mark (Roth). Now, they all want to be like Monacelli or Weber. A lot of the fundamentals have gone by the wayside."

Just because Roth's style worked best for him is no guarantee that it's right for you. "When I first came on Tour, I thought a lot about generating as much power as I could," McDowell relates. "Now I think about rolling my shots as well as I can. Doing that gives me maximum hitting power. Amleto changed his game. He has fewer revs now but a far better roll. You don't see unleashed revs very much anymore. It's far better to have a great roll. Bob (Benoit) is the ultimate."

Williams views Monacelli's evolution from a different perspective. According to Williams, Monacelli has obtained "greater control of his power, but he still has about as many revs as before. The difference is that they're more forward-type revolutions and less side-revs. That's why even though he crosses fewer boards, he has managed to maintain all of his ability to open up a lane while becoming more accurate."

Every player has his or her own individual strengths and weaknesses. McDowell admits that he doesn't have the natural great release of a Mark Baker, a Pete Weber, or a Rick Steelsmith. "Those guys," he raves, "have such great lift and turn that they make it look effortless."

One of McDowell's strengths is that his legs are among the most powerful in the PBA. With optimum footwork and balance, he fully exploits his physical assets.

His secret to maximizing leverage at the point of release is his consistent timing. "I delay my pushaway until my second step. That feels the most comfortable to me. My first step is very small," McDowell says.

"My approach is fairly compact. I'm only 5'8". When I used a longer approach, I found myself carrying the ball during parts of my armswing instead of allowing it to swing more freely. So I now start in front of the dots."

Although he's been occasionally mislabeled as a power player, McDowell thinks his game falls evenly between power and style. While most of what he does conforms to a traditional approach, his pushaway is slightly unorthodox.

In the address position, he holds the ball slightly below the waist. When he puts the ball into motion during his second step, McDowell pushes it forward and upward. "When my arm is extended forward, the ball is at about chest height," he relates. While doing so requires more

McDowell pushes his ball upward at the start for greater ball speed. (Photo by Steve Spatafore)

muscle power than the typical pushaway, McDowell has little trouble achieving a free armswing once the pushaway ends. The higher pushaway creates a longer armswing, which generates more momentum and power, McDowell believes.

McDowell acknowledges that his release is effective even if it isn't the envy of his peers. Some pros emphatically release the ball onto the lane. Perhaps the best analogy is TV commentator Nelson Burton's comparison of Monacelli's release to how one starts a power lawn mower. In contrast, McDowell is noted for his smoothness.

Many amateurs either throw the ball forward (or upward) or drop the ball into the lane. A far better alternative is to let it descend gradually as you release it. "Ideally," McDowell offers, "I want my ball to hit the lane the way an airplane lands on a runway. When David Ozio, Marshall Holman, Bob Benoit, or Pete Weber bowls, you don't even hear the ball as it lands on the lane.

One trait that all great contemporary players share is a first-rate release. (Photo by Steve Spatafore)

"I let go at the bottom of my swing. It's important that my thumb exits early. I have a relaxed grip. After my thumb is out, my fingers extend through the ball and toward the pins. I make a concerted effort to reach out toward my target. Throughout my entire delivery, all of my energies and concentration are toward that target. It's like having tunnel vision."

Perhaps the biggest misnomer in bowling is that the player who imparts an outstanding release is said to have gotten great "lift" on the ball. "Lift" implies an upward motion. Nothing could be further from reality.

To impart "lift" you don't "lift" anything: not your head, not your eyes (which remain riveted on your target until long after the conclusion of your delivery), and cer-

"Lift" comes from the fingers. (Photo by Steve Spatafore)

tainly not the ball. Your fingers must come through the
ball and be moving forward. States McDowell: "A major
problem that I share with many players is that I have a
tendency to hit up on the ball during my release. That's
probably because I grew up bowling on drier lanes that
demanded that I get the ball down the lane. I've worked
very hard at trying to roll the ball more smoothly."

McDowell's timing is slightly late. He estimates that
90 percent of PBA Touring pros finish their footwork before executing their release. Doing so adds leverage and
power as long as the timing isn't excessively late.

Perhaps the most powerful strike ball during the early
half of the 1990s belonged to Bob Vespi. McDowell studied
the Floridian's game and discovered an unconventional
approach. McDowell relates: "Bob is lanky and loose,
which is a great physique for his style. He has a big cup of
his wrist, and he comes up the back of the ball during his
release. There's a big bend in the elbow of his bowling
arm."

Like many power-oriented bowlers, Vespi's spare
shooting doesn't exactly inspire comparisons to that of
Williams or Ferraro. McDowell likens Vespi to a home-run
hitter whose big swing causes him to strike out a lot (of
course, in bowling, striking out is nice, but not when you donate marks by missing easy spares or by leaving far too
many difficult splits).

> **Ninety percent of pros finish their footwork before executing their release. Doing so adds leverage and power.**

"No matter how many strikes I throw, I wouldn't earn
a whole lot of money if I didn't make my spares," McDowell says.

There's little doubt who would prevail on the majority
of conditions if one gave Vespi and McDowell 100 shots
apiece with the winner being determined solely by who
threw the most strikes.

However, every triple is negated by a single open. McDowell's ability to also keep the ball in play means that he doesn't get in nearly as much trouble on most of his poorer shots as do the ultra-crankers. And McDowell's string of 300 games are proof positive that one doesn't have to rev it up to produce big numbers.

THE BENOIT METHOD

Bob Benoit's smooth style allows him to play the power game without a typical power player's delivery. He rolls the ball slowly and doesn't have a single herky-jerky motion throughout his entire delivery. Whereas an ultra-power type might accelerate his hand as he releases the shot, Benoit caresses the ball onto the lane.

To hear Benoit describe his movements, one would think he was anything but a power player. "I try to get my hand going at my target, I always walk toward my target, and my armswing is always right in line," he says. He's usually close to being in time, which sets him apart from the plant-and-shoot crowd of crankers such as Bob Vespi, Chris Warren, Kelly Coffman, and Ron Palombi, Jr.

In many ways, Benoit has the best of both worlds. He's as smooth as any of the shot-makers, which increases his accuracy, yet his carrying power ranks right near the top. His secret is what's known as "heavy roll." That allows his shots to achieve two often-contradictory objectives: They drive through the deck with little or no deflection, yet the pins aren't sent skyward. His ability to keep the lower-numbered pins close to the lane surface makes for fewer taps.

Many of us suffer from the solid 10 pin (lefties from the ringing 7 pin) because the 6 pin (4 pin for southpaws) flies around the neck of the corner pin. Given that the base of each pin is much wider than the neck, it's only logical that the lower the trajectory of the sticks, the less likely they are to miss those in the back row.

As we learned in the Introduction, it wasn't always so. The Bob Benoit who failed early in his pro career isn't to be mistaken for the guy who might have the best strike ball on the pro Tour.

In contrast to McDowell, Benoit virtually drops the ball into his armswing. (Photo by Steve Spatafore)

"In the past I threw the ball off of my heel," he acknowledges. "Instead of creating leverage by having my body weight over the knee of my sliding leg, I'd be off balance. The principle is the same as driving a golf ball or serving in tennis. As you release the ball, your momentum has to be moving forward."

The biggest shortcomings he used to suffer included pulling his head up off of his target (which caused him to rear up at the foul line) and pulling away from the ball with his hand on its side at the point of release. So poor was his weight distribution that he ruined the heels of several shoes.

The typical shot has a skid-roll-hook pattern. The ball skids through the front segment of the lane before it begins to roll. As it nears the pins, it begins to hook toward the pocket. Benoit's shots roll a lot earlier and hit with far more authority than they did in the past. He attributes this to his improved release.

"Before, my fingers were on the right side of the ball, and I'd turn my hand counterclockwise during my release," he says. "Now, my hand is underneath the ball, and I lift through it instead of coming around the side of it."

Benoit keeps his wrist in a cupped position. Says Benoit: "My release is almost as if I never had my thumb in the ball. It feels like I'm palming it. Once I feel my thumb exit, I pull my fingers toward the palm of my hand to get the lift that I need. My hand moves toward my target."

Benoit echoes McDowell's observations by noting: "When I mention 'lift,' most people think of standing up and going straight up. That's the worst thing you can do when letting go of your shot."

Asked what would happen if instead of rolling a bowling ball he used the same motion with only a coin in his palm, Benoit responded: "It would stay in my palm until after my release point. As my arm moved upward, the coin would fall to the left. By coming *slightly* around the ball, I get some side turn on my shot. If I didn't do that, my ball would roll too early, and it would roll out by the time it reached the pins."

His game is often compared to that of Del Ballard, Jr. Ballard, Benoit says, has a more pronounced acceleration of hand speed on his downswing and during the release. Ballard doesn't cup his wrist as much as Benoit, thus allowing him to use a higher backswing. Combined with faster feet, it means that Ballard's ball goes farther down the lane before it begins to hook. As such, Ballard has an edge on Benoit on a very dry condition (when the lanes hook at lot). Benoit enjoys an advantage on an oilier surface.

Hand acceleration requires the use of more muscle than does Benoit's method. Like Ballard, Warren and Holman also increase their hand speed prior to and during their release. Their styles, while extremely successful for them, are difficult for the occasional bowler to duplicate consistently.

When teaching others to bowl, Benoit uses the analogy of an airplane landing on a runway. His technique is such that he never intentionally lofts his shots. "When everything is in sync and I'm throwing my best, you can't hear my ball hit the lane," says Benoit. "When I'm off my game, the ball is lofted and it often bounces slightly to either side after having hit the lane."

Although his is a predominantly conventional style, there are some quirks in Benoit's game. He holds the ball below waist height during his address. His pushaway is forward and downward. He is still in his slide during his release, which is fine on most lanes but not recommended when the approaches are very slippery.

Benoit bends his elbow during his backswing. Not until it becomes straight as the arm begins its forward motion does Benoit's swing stop using excessive muscle.

The ideal shot lands on a lane in a similar manner to an airplane landing on a runway. (Photo by Steve Spatafore)

Not a good technique, you say? In Benoit's case, breaking the "loose armswing" axiom during the backswing works.

"The bend in my elbow helps alleviate the stress on my (cupped) wrist," Benoit explains. "Doing so allows the strength in my forearm to be used. My brother, Rick, throws the ball a lot like me except that his arm is straight during the entire delivery. He has had a lot of very extreme wrist problems. He's told me of sharp pains during his downswing that make it difficult for him just to hold onto the ball."

Bob Benoit's style isn't for everybody. It took him several years to refine his game.

He was the object of much derision back home when he spent the first six months rolling a 10-pound ball. It took him another half of a year to build up to using a 16-pound ball. Although he says that "people laughed at me,"

Benoit knew that the smart move wasn't to use a heavy ball before his body was ready to accept the stress.

"When you lift weights, you don't start out at 200 pounds," is his logic. "You begin with light weights and build up to heavier ones. I had to strengthen my muscles gradually so I wouldn't damage my wrist or elbow."

To Benoit, being on the "right track" has a different connotation than it might to the rest of us. As with all good bowlers, the same portion of Bob's bowling ball comes in contact with the lane on every strike shot. After minimal use, normal wear and tear becomes visibly apparent. The sections of the ball that touch the lane are said to be the "track."

Just by observing a player's ball, one can learn a lot about that bowler's game. You can study your track to discover the diameter of your ring.

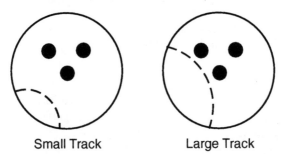

Small Track　　　　　　Large Track

The diagram above reveals two diametrically opposed possibilities. The ball on the left has a very small track. It won't drive through the pins with efficiency. In contrast, the track of the ball on the right is a far greater size. This Benoit-like alternative is murder on pins.

In bowling lingo, Benoit now enjoys a much "higher roll" than in the past. The track is just outside of his thumb and finger holes. Evidence of the anemic strike ball that he tossed in his early days was a track several inches removed from the holes.

Another player with a high roll is Pete Weber. Like

Benoit, Weber's track is just outside the thumb and finger holes. Pete's famous dad, Dick, excelled in an era in which the full roller was the most prominent. Its track cut between the finger and thumb holes. To the best of Benoit's knowledge, no current pro uses a full roller. "It just doesn't hit hard enough," he says.

The popular three-quarter roller sees the track about one to two inches away from the holes. Ideally, Benoit suggests, the distance of the track from the thumb hole should be identical to how far it's removed from the nearer of the finger holes. Many lower-average players have a track that's considerably closer to the thumb hole than to the finger hole. They need to concentrate on staying behind the ball longer during their release to get more power.

Benoit's spare-shooting method of flattening his wrist to roll a relatively straight shot produces a track similar to the one he used to have before he revamped his game. "Shooting spares comes naturally to me," he offers, "because I only have to do what I did before I learned how to roll a powerful ball."

Benoit has a double advantage. He has the carrying power to match any of his Tour rivals. Unlike most power players, however, he began by rolling a straight ball, which means that "when I learned how to hook a ball I still had the mentality of the straight player. I still look at a target. I'll pick a zone that's two to three boards wide.

"I see a lot of kids who grow up hooking the ball who just stand to one area, twist it up, and throw the ball to the right. If their shot misses the pocket, they become lost. They have no idea about how to adjust."

The more boards that one crosses, the greater the invitation to disaster. A straight shot is aimed at the pocket, and a moderate hook is thrown up the boards, while the big hook is initially projected toward the channel. When the oil pattern becomes unpredictable and the conditions are the most challenging, the bowler most likely to succeed is the one who combines the power of a moderate hook shot with a high degree of accuracy.

States Benoit: "When you throw a big hook, there is more chance of a big error. The more you aim the ball away from the pocket, the harder it is to be consistent. Big hook balls leave some awful split conglomerations."

That statement rings even more true on Tour conditions in which a so-called out of bounds exists. The PBA lane-maintenance crew often intentionally floods the outside few boards of a lane with a heavy allotment of oil. The shot that misses wide of its target on the Tour doesn't receive the forgiveness that the big hook player gets on many house conditions.

"If there is no out of bounds on a house condition, the player who hooks the ball has the advantage," asserts Benoit. "When one of them misses by three to five boards to the right, they still have a chance of getting a nine count. A guy who throws more straight who misses the target by that much will only get six or seven pins."

Bowling centers have a vested interest in maintaining high-scoring conditions. The perception among proprietors is that bowlers prefer to bowl where their averages will be the highest. Where there is no out of bounds, typically the crankers enjoy an edge.

"Where I live in Topeka," notes Benoit, "junior bowlers brag about how much they can hook the ball. They just run up to the line, plant their foot, and wing it. Their head goes to the left and their body falls to the right. When the pins fly all over the place, it is impressive to watch."

Benoit says that achieving power has become "something of a macho thing."

Aside from the problem of inconsistent performance, Benoit worries that such players will pay a price in the future. "People tend to forget that the ball weighs a lot. It's one thing to kick a soccer ball hard or to drive a golf ball 300 yards. It's another thing to really hit up on something that can be as much as 16 pounds. Sooner or later many of these kids are going to blow out a knee, an elbow, and/or the wrist and its connecting tendons.

"If I wanted to, I can rev it up with a Dave Wodka or a Kelly Coffman," he says, alluding to two of the Tour's young ultra-power players. "From week to week and year to year, which type of game and which player is going to make the most money?"

Benoit typically earns far more than Wodka and Coffman combined. A Coffman strike might elicit more "oohs" and "aahs" from spectators, but "oohs" and "aahs" don't pay the rent.

Good timing, however, does help in that regard. Benoit varies his delivery. He may use as few as five steps or as many as seven. He adds strides when he thinks that he's "pushing the ball away too quickly and getting my footwork ahead of the ball. I correct that by slowing down. I take shorter and slower steps."

Other players might actually increase their speed by adding one or more strides. They do so by also increasing the distance from the foul line where they start in the address position. Benoit adds steps without adding distance from the foul line.

The 5'9" veteran always uses the entire approach. "It's how I get my momentum," he states. "I don't have a big backswing. Like Marshall Holman and Del Ballard, Jr., I create my momentum with my feet."

All three are always hunched from the waist with their shoulders forward so that each is over his sliding knee during the release.

Like McDowell, the first of Benoit's five steps is small and is used for timing purposes. "I just pick my foot up a little bit. When it comes back down I start my next step as I push the ball forward. If I go to six steps I hold the ball still until after my second step. When I use seven steps the ball doesn't move until my third step is done."

HOW BAKER COOKS

Even before Mark Baker starts his delivery, it's clear that one of the Tour's most imposing physical specimens has made some adjustments to compensate in a sport in which being big is a disadvantage. "There are not a lot of guys my size who can bowl well," admits the 6'4" star.

"The hardest thing for me is that other guys can bowl all-out, while I have to tone everything down. The center of gravity for shorter players is lower, so it takes less effort for them to have a good knee bend. It's much harder for me to have a good knee bend to roll the ball smoothly. I have to be in time.

"If I had the same foot speed as Marshall Holman, I'd throw the ball through the back of the building. If my swing were as big as that of Pete Weber, I'd be throwing shots at 27 or 28 miles per hour. Chris Warren has to put all that he has into every shot. I have to take something off.

"In my opinion, bowling is the only sport I know in which you're penalized for being big and strong. It's as if someone said to Jose Canseco, 'That ball that you just hit went 480 feet, so we're only going to give you a single for it.' "

During his address, Baker has his feet a few inches apart. He says that's a "more natural stance" to promote balance. Besides, he notes, "you don't walk with your feet together, so why start out that way?"

A five-step player, Baker begins with a short slide "to get me moving. After that, I walk naturally. Most of the better pros have fast feet. The faster that you move, the easier it is to stay down at the line. You shouldn't run up to the line, but you should definitely walk faster than you would on a sidewalk."

He holds the ball just under belt height during his address. His pushaway, like Benoit's, is out and down. To do otherwise at his size would create a very long arm-swing that would bring about excessive ball speed. The Baker backswing comes within a few inches of shoulder height.

Because he's so big and strong, Baker's backswing doesn't need to be as high as those of many smaller men who must bring their ball above their shoulders to generate sufficient ball speed.

One of the laws of bowling that Baker never forgets is the maxim that steady results come only when you keep your head steady. Explains Baker: "In any sport it's easier to hit your target when your eyes remain focused on it and your head doesn't move. I was taught as a kid to pretend that I had a glass of water on top of my head and that I was to concentrate on not spilling a single drop."

Like McDowell, Baker thinks that most of his power derives from his legs. The former basketball player says that his deep knee bend at the point of release is but part of the equation.

Asserts Baker: "The step before the slide is very important. I call it the 'drive step.' Nelson Burton calls it the 'pivot step.' As my right foot pushes off, I drive forward instead of upwards. That helps to propel me into my slide. That's one thing that all of the top pros do well and what virtually every amateur fails to do."

Baker's nature is to throw the ball hard. He makes a concerted effort to avoid doing so except on very dry lanes. He's master of that condition because it's the only situation in which he's rewarded for fast ball speed.

As for a Baker tip, here's his advice on following through: "I try to keep my ring finger in the direction of my target for as long as possible. The most important thing is to keep your head looking at the target. So many people want to look up to see what the pins will be doing that they rear up at the line and hit up on their shot.

"Your ball, when properly released, creates area. If
you keep your head down and hit your target, you will get
to the pocket all 12 times."

*Baker credits much of his 300-game success to taking advantage of his
leg power to maximize leverage during his drive step and his slide/
release. (Photo by Steve Spatafore)*

THE WILLIAMS WAY

Despite his fantastic consistency, Walter Ray Williams isn't one to blow his own horn. "I'm pretty much a self-taught player, so I don't have textbook form although it's probably fairly close," he says.

Williams, too, walks the tightrope between power and accuracy. "I use a lot of power, more so than many fans think," Williams states. "Although my strike ball may not be as powerful as that of some pros, it is still more than sufficient to get the job done on most lane conditions. On every strike ball, I'm putting 90 percent of what I've got into it. Once in a while, I will put 100 percent into it. Some of the other players say that I just about jump out of my shoes."

He accelerates his armswing prior to a release. As Williams lets go of the ball, his body position is very orthodox. His follow-through is unique. His left (nonbowling) arm flies behind his back ("it looks like it's dislocated"), and his right leg kicks behind his body. While those traits would cost him style points if bowling were scored as is gymnastics, neither of those quirks makes him less productive. The reason is that his big kick and his left arm's movements help maintain his balance as he's delivering the shot. Any sacrifice of balance occurs long after he has released the ball.

Just two inches shorter than Baker, Williams uses long strides. He says that's a carryover from horseshoes. Being big, in his opinion, isn't such a crippling disadvantage that it can't be overcome. The reason that so many stars are on the diminutive side, he says, "might be that the shorter fellows go into bowling because you don't need a certain body type to become a star, while many of the bigger guys have been sought out by the other sports."

The successes of Weber, Monacelli, Ferraro, Wayne Webb, and McDowell make a compelling case that, on the lanes at least, less can be more. Despite that, Williams proves that being 6′2″ doesn't preclude excelling at the PBA level.

Like Baker, Williams has exceptional timing. His footwork gives him outstanding leverage at the point of release. Williams reports enjoying "a fairly high roll." The track comes within three-fourths of an inch of the nearer finger hole. It's approximately half an inch from the thumb hole.

As with most big men, he uses the entire approach. He's a master at changing releases and ball speeds. When trying to roll his shots slowly to achieve more hook, he will begin his delivery closer to the foul line. Doing that slows down his feet, decreasing his arm speed.

Using less speed is usually the best strategy when bowling on heavy oil. But Williams cautions that on occasion, he's noticed a correlation between less velocity and rollout. If you're hitting the pocket but the ball is rolling out so it's not driving through the pins, try using a bit more speed, a more porous ball, more of an outside line, or a combination of the three.

Both Walter Ray and Mark Williams (no relation) have reputations for being able to make major adjustments by altering the release. When Walter Ray Williams wants to reduce his hook, he places his hand on the side of the ball in a suitcase-like grip. Lifting his fingers straight upward when releasing from that position produces some hook. To impart more hook, he places his hand underneath the ball.

Arguably one of the strongest men on the Tour, Williams nevertheless shuns the high-revving style of the crankers. "I'm a lot stronger than Chris Warren, but he can out-hook me with no problem," Williams says. "I can't put the same rotation on the ball as him even though I must outweigh Chris by 70 pounds."

While the above might seem to suggest that Warren, not Williams, is the more likely candidate to string strikes,

It's not pretty but Williams's patented follow-through gets the job done. (Photo by Steve Spatafore)

the record shows that Williams more than holds his own in that category.

Without getting into a complicated physics lesson, suffice it to say that the ball's ability to drive through the pins isn't only achieved by having a more pronounced hook.

One factor as to why Williams's seemingly less-powerful ball can match the power players strike for strike is that there is a point at which additional power can become counterproductive.

Among the leaves that Williams is less likely to suffer than the crankers are the 9-pin spare or the 4-9 and the rip 7-10 splits. A right-handed power player is less likely than

Williams to be faced with a 10-pin or the occasional deflection split (5-7 or the 8-10).

Which brings us back to how we began this chapter: discussing the tradeoff between power and accuracy. On most surfaces, the ultra-power players carry more off-hits, but the more conventional types hit the pocket more often.

It's interesting that a list of all-time 300-game leaders in PBA competition includes many bowlers who one doesn't associate with great carry. Steve Wunderlich, the

Although primarily noted for being a smooth stylist, Steve Wunderlich can produce 300s with anyone. (Photo by Steve Spatafore)

ultimate stylist, comes to mind. Williams, with his record-tying three perfect games in a single tournament, provides further evidence that sending pins flying may be exciting, but it doesn't always provide a competitive edge.

To obtain maximum carry, look at the qualities that most power players and stylists share: consistent timing, a good release, balance at the line for maximum leverage, and holding your head steady throughout.

We also suggest avoiding the pitfall that hinders many league bowlers. Don't be so awed by the way that your favorite pro throws his or her shots that you attempt to do something you're not capable of duplicating.

There are as many different styles on the Tour as there are body types. You will probably discover what's best suited to your needs by trial and error coupled with learning how to achieve a balance between power and accuracy.

3

EQUIPMENT

In no other popular American game does having the optimum equipment play as big a role as it does on the lanes. We know that today's bowler is 25 times more likely to produce a 300 than were the players of 30 years ago. Even if contemporary tenpin participants make the dubious claim of an across-the-board doubling in ability over their predecessors, that still leaves more than a twelvefold improvement unexplained.

To discover the reason, you need look no farther than the shelves of your nearest pro shop. Today's equipment, and bowling balls in particular, is light-years ahead of the 1960s models. The advancements have been so significant that they may be detrimental to the game. Rolling strikes is so much easier that countless amateurs with serious flaws in their games are still able to carry high averages.

One would think that as scores have risen dramatically, there would be a commensurate rise in participation. After all, who among us shuns an activity that provides great ego fulfillment?

In fact, the opposite has been the case. Far fewer

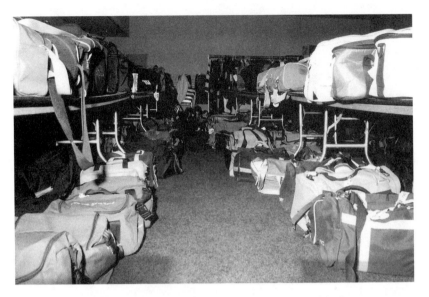

Hundreds of bowling bags and balls fill the PBA paddock at every tournament site. (Photo by Steve Spatafore)

people bowl in leagues today than they did in the 1960s and 1970s. And far fewer league bowlers take the time to practice as much as did the players of the immediate post-pinboy era.

Why practice when you can drop a ball on your downswing and it still hooks into the pocket? Why practice when a superior ball can overcome a poor release?

Unlike our golf or tennis brethren, only a few bowlers feel compelled to spend many hours working on their skills. Although pros believe that's a mistake, there's no denying that the advancements in equipment have given the lazy player a shortcut to respectability.

If averaging 170–180 is your goal, you will need only the right ball and shoes plus a modicum of talent. You may even roll a perfect game or two without having to upgrade your skills.

The smart and ambitious bowler knows that marrying serious practice with ability and combining both with top-of-the-line equipment is the best formula for success. The same $130 urethane ball that can add 10 pins to an average player's game can add 15 to 20 sticks to the scores of more-polished bowlers.

Either way, those antiquated plastic or rubber balls just can't cut it anymore. Using the outdated models and trying to match an opponent with a urethane ball strike for strike makes about as much sense as challenging a driver in a Ferrari to a race when you're behind the wheel of a station wagon.

American Bowling Congress regulations designed to maintain the integrity of the game have consistently fallen short of their objective. Except on the pro Tours, where lane conditions are made intentionally more challenging to offset equipment advancements, records are falling like so many Riddick Bowe opponents.

Still, regulators in Wisconsin are trying to keep some control. The latest legal standards for bowling balls as of press time were announced by ABC/WIBC (Women's International Bowling Congress) executive Joyce Deitch. She stated: "The . . . implementation of these . . . specifications completes this phase of the committee's work on bowling balls in relation to the System of Bowling. The equipment specifications department and manufacturers shared information to ensure all specifications are in the best interest of the bowlers and the industry."

And just what did Deitch's group decide? In order to be kosher, from 1993 onward all 13- to 16-pound balls must have a Radius of Gyration of at least 2.43 but not more than 2.8 inches. The Coefficient of Restitution would henceforth be in the .65 to .78 range. And the Coefficient of Friction could be anywhere from nothing up to .39.

Say what?

The above rules strike us like the reply to the riddle: What happens when you cross an elephant with a rhinoceros? (Answer: El-if-I-know).

Don't fret if you have no idea as to what Deitch and her colleagues have mandated. Very few bowlers have a clue as to what it all means. What we do know is that equipment is becoming increasingly sophisticated. Equipment discussions among Touring pros include drilling terms that sound like a foreign language. Charts that list the characteristics of each ball seemingly offer more options than does a menu in a Chinese restaurant.

The good news is that it's OK if you think that "negative weight" is a lunar phenomenon or the result of a great diet. There's no problem if the only "pin" that you've heard about comes in groups of ten (your ball also has a pin to help your pro locate the placement of the interior weight block). You need not know anything about axis weight or the relationship of the track to your ball's weight block to exploit the many recent advancements.

WHERE TO BUY?

What you must possess are the qualities required to be a good consumer. The key is to discover a pro shop whose proprietor is knowledgeable. After all, you don't have to have an understanding of how a transmission works to know that the engine in a Mercedes-Benz is superior to that in a Yugo.

Who drills your ball is much more important than which ball you select. Notes Mark Baker: "A lot of pro shops shouldn't be open. Just because somebody put up a shingle saying 'Pro Shop' doesn't mean the guy inside knows what he's doing. Some of them couldn't average 180 if they keep score themselves. In every Pro-Am, I see amateurs whose hands resemble hamburger meat."

Your best bet comes from word of mouth. Talk to the better players in your area to learn where they take their business. The odds are that the overwhelming majority of higher-average bowlers patronize the area pro with the greatest expertise.

As to buying a less-expensive ball at a sporting goods store, we have one word of advice: don't! To place your trust in someone who knows a little about all sports rather than a lot about bowling is as silly as asking your plumber instead of a stockbroker for advice on playing the market.

Bring your current ball or balls with you when buying a new one. An expert driller can see important clues as to the type of roll you have. You should know enough about your game and about the lane conditions where you normally compete so that the pro can take that information and combine it with his or her expertise to come up with the ball that's tailor-made for you.

Or, perhaps, no single ball is best for you all the time.

Why would anyone need more than one bowling ball? Because, like snowflakes, no two types are alike. You can buy ones that work best on heavy oil or ones made for light oil. You can buy one that's better suited for an inside line or one designed to play up the boards. You can buy ones that hook a lot, a little, or hardly at all. You can even buy ones that are designed to skid so that their tendency to minimize hook makes them more accurate. These are ideal for the types of spares that don't require carrying power.

The range of options broadens when you consider that you can alter your ball's characteristics by either polishing its surface or by using an abrasive (such as sandpaper) to increase the amount of friction between it and the lane. More on that later.

KNOWLEDGE IS THE KEY

The more options at your fingertips, the less adjusting you'll have to do with your physical game to compensate for a change in lane conditions. It's far easier to switch balls than to alter your hand or wrist position, strike line, or ball speed.

So complex is the topic of equipment that many observers think that learning how to respond to lane conditions is the most difficult adjustment that PBA rookies face. While many of the better newcomers possess the physical ability to compete at that level, the initiation period remains lengthy.

Marc McDowell set the PBA record for the most money earned by a freshman, but his total was little more than one-third of what that year's (1986) leading earner (Walter Ray Williams) claimed.

McDowell easily surpassed his first-year earnings in 1989, 1990, 1991, and 1992. Like all veteran pros, he has worked hard to hone his physical skills, but a bigger difference between the rookie McDowell and the veteran is his mental game.

From the start of his PBA career, it was clear that McDowell possessed outstanding concentration and a fairly even temperament. Much of his improvement came from learning about equipment options.

In the course of a calendar year, it's not unusual for some pros to use more than 100 different bowling balls in an ongoing trial-and-error quest to discover the secret formula that works best on that week's specific condition. That number might be even higher if PBA rules didn't limit competitors to a maximum of eight balls in the locker room at any one time.

Times have certainly changed from the days when everyone used the same kind of ball for several months and the only individualism involved drilling the finger holes to fit the owner's hand.

Until the late 1970s, bowlers treated a ball like a pair of shoes: You used it until it wore out and then you purchased a replacement. In this era when a simple $20 sneaker has evolved to become cross trainers that are pumped with air, it's little wonder that the $29.95 rubber bowling ball is extinct in favor of urethane models. The better of them usually cost $110–$140.

What does this mean to you, the amateur who is relatively serious about your bowling? By bringing your business to a top-class pro, you can gain a tremendous competitive edge. It's fairly common these days for higher-average league players to own at least one ball for dry lanes and another for oily ones. It's a good bet that if you give that bowler on your Christmas list a $100 pro shop gift certificate that he or she will have little problem putting it to good use.

The better that your game becomes, the better that your equipment will work.

Most ball manufacturers offer several versions of their top-of-the-line urethane balls. It's not enough to decide that you want to buy a Rhino, an Enforcer, a Hammer, an Angle, a U-Dot, a Turbo, or any of several other first-rate balls on the market. You have to decide which color you want.

No, the red one isn't meant to match your favorite Christmas outfit. It might be designed for use on oily lanes, while the black ball works well on dry surfaces and the tan one is for lanes that fall between the two extremes.

Ball colors aren't consistent from manufacturer to manufacturer. A blue ball of Company A might be its "hookingest" model, while Company B's blue model might be the hard-shell one designed to go straighter. To check, look for that chart on the wall of the pro shop.

Let's review what oil does. A generous application of lane conditioner reduces the amount of friction between your ball and the surface. That means that your shot won't hook nearly as much. A drier surface maximizes the lane-ball friction and, with it, the amount that your shot will hook.

Not only is the amount of oil an issue; so, too, is the length to which it is applied. "Short oil" means that the front end is conditioned while the back is dry (at least until carrydown becomes a factor)—more on that in our next chapter. "Long oil" means that the break point is delayed until your shot leaves the conditioned segment of the lane (which could be as far as 45 feet out of the 60-foot distance from the foul line to the headpin).

Because there are dozens of pros of comparable physical ability, equipment decisions can make the difference between winning and losing. Players gain a significant advantage by recognizing and countering the lane conditions a game, or even a few frames, sooner than their opponents. It's no wonder that we've all heard pros exclaim that bowling is "90 percent mental."

Sorry, guys, but it's not. If it were 90 percent mental, only 10 percent of them could defeat William Buckley, Jr. As we know, there's a big difference between the kegling skills of those on the firing line and those of the host of "Firing Line."

If all other things are equal, only then does bowling become 90 percent mental. You or I could know twice as much about equipment and have better concentration than Pete Weber, but I doubt we could give him a tough match. Buying the world's best ball will help anyone, but it won't make you a great player if you can't roll it correctly any more than the most expensive dress from the world's top fashion designer can make Roseanne Arnold look like Christie Brinkley.

Asserts Mark Baker: "I work harder on my game than I do on my equipment. The better that your game becomes, the better that your equipment will work. Find equipment that's comfortable, and then concentrate on becoming a better bowler. Mark Roth, Marshall Holman, Walter Ray

Williams, and Amleto Monacelli don't drill very many new balls. My advice is that you'll improve a lot more if you spend more time practicing than you do in the pro shop."

BUY SMART

It's easy for the amateur to assume that what ball he throws is more important than how he throws it. In the hands of a gifted player, the ball that is most compatible with that player's roll and line on that particular oil pattern can make a big difference. There are too many mediocre players who waste their money buying ball after ball as if it's only a matter of time before they hit on the one that will magically turn them into superior bowlers.

They should concentrate their energies in a more productive and less expensive direction. After all, the answer to that question of how one gets to Carnegie Hall isn't "buy a better violin." (For those of you behind on your aphorisms, the correct response is "practice, practice, practice.")

Does that mean that after you reach the 170-average plateau that you can't gain an edge through optimum use of equipment? Of course not. You can and you will, but, cautions Baker: "It's a lot easier to get to 180 than it is to go from 190 to 210. Equipment can help but the most important factors are having natural ability and working hard on your game."

He suggests: "Some people are into buying every new ball that comes on the market. Don't be the first guy to buy that new model because every company has had a couple of lemons."

Every company has also had some gems. Spending $140 for a ball, $125 for the best shoes, and another $50 or so on accessories will add pins to your average. Your first challenge is to get that average to at least the 170–180 range. Once that's accomplished, you have demonstrated an ability to achieve a certain degree of consistency. Because you are rolling most of your shots over the same part of the ball, you can take full advantage of the versatility that urethane offers.

URETHANE'S THE ONE

The one given is that on almost every condition, serious players will use a urethane ball. The advantage of urethane balls is that they grip the lane so well that they minimize shot deflection. The result is vastly superior carrying power for higher scoring.

With the research-and-development divisions of all the manufacturers working constantly to find better formulas, there is the chance that urethane—like rubber, plastic, and wood before it—will someday yield to a more effective surface. But as we write this, no other surface comes close to matching the quality of urethane.

Except on rare occasions when they use plastic balls on very dry lanes, pros rely exclusively on urethane equipment. Even on a dry surface, the ball of choice most of the time will be the shinier urethane model that was polished at the factory. It's designed to go farther down the lane before it starts to hook. So superior is urethane that rubber balls are virtually extinct and plastic ones are on the endangered-species list.

There might not be a player on either the LPBT or PBA Tour who knows more about equipment than does Bob Benoit. He operated one of the nation's finest pro shops for six years.

Benoit relates: "There are so many options that buying a bowling ball is like going into a restaurant whose menu has 10 pages of different types of hamburgers. It can be very confusing. A lot of people would come through the door and ask 'What's the best ball on the market?' That's like asking, 'What's the best car?' Some people prefer GM products, others like Fords, and others swear by the imports. It's a matter of personal preference. The top-of-the-line balls of all of the major companies are good."

Benoit suggests that if you're happy with your current ball, consider buying other balls from that manufacturer. Each company offers a range of options.

Unless you have unlimited resources (and a very strong back required to carry several 16-pound balls into the center), Benoit recommends owning no more than a few balls. Buy smart so that you give yourself equipment flexibility for more options.

Benoit explains: "I have seen players come into a center with six different balls and every one of them is the hookingest ball from a different manufacturer. They've gotten totally confused. It's made bowling more difficult than it should be."

Players in the 170–190 range should own two or, at most, three balls. Those at 190+ might benefit from owning four to six. Either way, warns Benoit, "You can get too many balls with too many different weights and surfaces."

PLAY FAVORITES

Designate one ball as your favorite. Pick the one that works best more often than the others. Use that ball as

Baker's advice on balls:
play favorites.
(Photo by Steve Spatafore)

your reference point. Asserts Baker: "Everyone should have a favorite ball so that you know how it will react on every lane condition. You base everything off of that.

"A lot of the guys on Tour like to use a straight ball and make it hook," says Baker. "I like to go the other way."

After you have warmed up and are satisfied that you are throwing good shots, you can "read" the lane. You'll know if your preferred ball is working or whether you need more, or less, hook. By understanding the characteristics of all of your balls compared to your favorite one, you can decide which other one to try next.

If you want a ball to hook more, apply an abrasive to its surface.

There are times when you'll find that your "straight ball" isn't hooking enough but that your "hooking ball" is flying. What to do?

You can change the characteristics of any ball on the spot. If you want a ball to hook more, apply an abrasive to its surface. Using sandpaper is a favorite way to "rough up" the surface so that there is more friction between the ball and the lane. Although it's possible to "sand" a ball by hand, a far better method is to have your pro do it for you by placing the ball on a spinner machine.

Conversely, you can decrease friction (and, with it, hook) by making the surface shinier. Virtually every bowling center has a ball-polishing machine. That extra layer of coating will make the ball skid more and hook less.

In most cases if you plan on owning two balls, Benoit usually recommends buying one that hooks a lot and one that hooks very little. You're now ready to compete on a dry or an oily lane.

The reason that Benoit said "usually" is because you might bowl in a center that is virtually always either very heavily or very lightly oiled. If that's the case, you might never get to use that second ball. As a knowledgeable pro,

Benoit knows the characteristics of all of the bowling centers in his area. If you've picked the right person, your pro will, too. Listen to his or her advice.

As noted, scratch bowlers may benefit from owning four or more balls. Baker suggests having a "cheater" ball, a two-piece ball, a shiny ball, and a ball for average conditions.

The "cheaters" came on the scene in the early 1990s. They are officially known as "reactive resin balls." Although they overreact on most lane surfaces, they are absolutely devastating when the conditions favor their use.

Observes Baker: "When they do work, they are simply amazing. They go long in the oil and then they grab the dry boards very hard. The scientist who invented them knew what he was doing."

McDowell cautions that they are only suited for some bowlers on some lane conditions. Observes McDowell, "They are so reactive that they magnify whatever the bowler does." That includes magnifying a change in ball speed, release, or line, so you'd better have obtained a degree of consistency before plunking down $140 for one of these babies.

Like most modern urethane balls, reactive resin balls have a two-piece construction.

According to former pro shop proprietor Benoit, the more even and stronger roll of the two-piece ball has made it far more common than balls of three-piece construction. The latter skid longer and don't drive as well on heavy oil. As such, they are best on a dry lane when it's important for the ball to skid a significant distance before breaking.

Baker cautions that there are no hard-and-fast rules regarding what you decide to add to your arsenal. The key is to gain as many options as possible so that you can make major adjustments with your equipment and have to make only minor adjustments in your physical game.

WEIGHTY MATTERS

No ball, no matter how good, will work for you unless the pro who drills it knows what he's doing. The position of the pin in a two-piece ball, explains Benoit, indicates the location of the weight block to its static center. The static center is defined as the place where one can drill the holes so that the weights are symmetrical. An experienced pro can locate the angle of the pin to the static center by weighing it on a special scale.

Some balls are constructed with their pin within an inch of the static center. Known as "pin in," they roll earlier with less back-end flip. Pin out refers to a pin that's two to four inches removed from the static center. These skid farther with a greater amount of back-end flip. They're extremely effective on a dry lane.

The pin of the ball. (Photo by Steve Spatafore)

Benoit has learned how a ball's characteristics can be altered by moving the location of the holes in relation to the weight block. The good news is that a knowledgeable pro can maximize the effectiveness of your new ball. The flip side is that the incompetent pro shop proprietor can have the opposite effect.

Benoit has met "at least a half dozen" house "pros" who didn't know the significance of the pin. "In one Pro-Am, I bowled with an amateur whose ball had its pin at 10 o'clock. His shots rolled out early so there was no flip on the back end.

"He couldn't figure out why he couldn't get his ball to hook or to carry. I told him it was because his ball was drilled for a left-handed player. He wrote to tell me that after going back home, he found a pro who knew what he was doing. He had the ball plugged and redrilled the right way. He said it made a huge difference in his game."

Taking your business to a Benoit-caliber pro in the first place is worth the effort. Although neither you nor I may fully understand his explanation that follows, it does point out how much expertise is required to drill equipment properly.

Here's Benoit on pin placement: "You have to take into consideration where the track (on the ball) is found. I have a high track. It's about one-half inch from the thumb hole and three-quarters of an inch from the finger holes. I prefer my pin around 2 or 3 o'clock.

"If a customer comes in with a ball in which their track is one-quarter of an inch from the thumb hole but three to three-and-a-half inches from the finger holes, I immediately know that their ball won't roll as heavily as does mine. They need to get their shot into an earlier roll to create that flip on the back end. So they need their pin to be around 4 or 5 o'clock."

Once again, it's not important that you or I memorize Bob's pin formula. It is important that we come to appre-

ciate the need to take our business to a pro who's knowledgeable. In Benoit's opinion, "less than 50 percent" of pro
shop operators have what he considers to be an "adequate"
understanding of their profession.

If the person who drilled your equipment in the past
wasn't doing a good job, it's quite possible that your new
ball that's been drilled by a competent pro may feel too
tight. The finger holes should be fairly snug. Finger holes
that are too large cause you to squeeze the ball so that you
won't drop it. That, in turn, makes it virtually impossible
to execute a smooth and powerful release.

Should the finger holes of your new ball be painfully
tight, ask your pro to make them slightly larger. But if
they just feel a bit uncomfortable because you have become accustomed to having excessive room, you should
allow yourself time to become acclimated to that new feel.

Unbeknownst to many bowlers, the diameter of your
thumb varies. Changes in temperature affect it, and it also
will become larger or smaller after having thrown a number of shots. That's why your pro should make that hole
sufficiently generous to fit properly when your thumb size
is the greatest.

Ask your pro to show you how to insert (and remove)
tape in the thumb hole to gain a proper fit at times when
it's less than its maximum size. This is an important step,
since having a comfortable grip is a key ingredient toward
executing a good release.

Your pro can position the holes to place your ball s
weight off-center. For example, Baker prefers to have a
combination of what's known as positive side weight, top
weight, and finger weight.

The last means that the ball's center of gravity is
nearer to the finger holes than to the thumb. Top weight
means there is more weight near the top than the bottom
of your ball. Positive side weight means that as the ball

rolls down the lane, the inside of the ball (the left side of a right-hander's ball or the right side of a left-hander's ball) has more weight than does the outside.

The weight combinations that Baker uses allow his shots to go farther down the lane before hooking and to make "a harder flip" in the back end. In other words, the hooking action of his ball is enhanced in the area of the lane just before the shot contacts the pins.

In combination, Baker's preferences are categorized as "positive weight." In contrast, "negative weight" would cause a shot to roll sooner and to hook far less dramatically in the back end. These are also sometimes called "rolling weights." Examples are thumb weight, bottom weight, and negative side weight.

"Skidding weights" are the same as "positive weight." As their name implies, they are designed to make your shot skid farther down the lane before "flipping" into a powerful pin-shattering roll.

Baker owns two two-piece balls. One is drilled over the label, while the other has a weight shift so it will react more violently on the back end of the lane. He has a three-piece ball that's easier to keep in play when excessive carrydown makes hitting the pocket a more challenging proposition. He has several shiny balls and dull balls that are drilled slightly differently to give him more options.

Most important, Baker knows the differing characteristics of each. As Benoit observes, "Not all dull two-piece balls have a similar roll."

Comparing three-piece construction to a two-piece ball, Benoit says the latter carries better on a dry lane, the former on heavy oil. When the lanes are dry, the three-piece allows you to get your shot farther down the lane before starting its break. On an oily lane, a dull two-piece ball has a shorter skid and a heavier roll to create hook and movement toward the pocket.

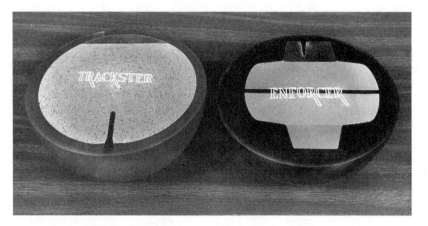

A two-piece (left) vs. a three-piece (right) ball construction. (Photo by Steve Spatafore)

HOW MUCH SHOULD YOUR BALL WEIGH?

Speaking of negative weights, there's nothing more negative than using a ball that's too heavy or too light for your needs. Generally speaking, you should use the heaviest ball that you can comfortably control.

Most men use the legal limit of a 16-pound ball. Women's balls tend to range from 12 pounds to 16. Body weight or gender isn't as important as strength. Don't feel pressured into using a heavier ball if it's hard for you to control.

Using a ball that is too heavy makes it difficult to have a loose armswing and to be consistently accurate. In addition, you'll tire quicker.

A ball that's too light also has many disadvantages. It deflects more when hitting the pins, causing poorer carry. You may have a tendency to fling (rather than roll) your shots.

While we can't provide a magic formula for you, your pro should be able to help you make the right decision.

Incidentally, not all pros go the 16-pound route. Benoit rolled his historic 300 game with a 15-pound ball. "I used a 16-pound ball for about a year and a half after I changed my game," he relates. "I was leaving a lot of 4 pins, 9 pins, and 4-9 splits. I had myself filmed to find the problem. I discovered that the pins were airborne and that with my roll and relatively slow speed, my shots weren't deflecting at all. I experimented with a lighter ball in the hope that it would deflect just enough to solve that problem but not so much as to cause other problems. It worked."

In fact, Benoit used a 14½-pound ball to average 229.1 for the week as he finished third in the 1989 Showboat Atlantic City Open.

On conditions that cause his shots to hook a lot, Benoit might decide to go a bit lighter. By using less than the legal limit, the 130-pound Benoit finds it less strenuous to throw the ball faster, when needed.

IT FITS LIKE A GLOVE

A proper fit is essential. Despite his considerable size, the 6'4" Baker has a span of 4⅝" to 4¾". He debunks the myth that there should be a chasm between the thumb and finger holes of a ball to maximize power. In fact, an excessive span can cause injury.

Asserts Baker: "I feel that you should be able to place a pencil between your palm and the ball. Having a relaxed and comfortable grip is far more valuable than getting a bit of extra power from a longer but uncomfortable span."

Don't let someone convince you that the potentially painful elongated span is a necessary evil to obtain maximum power. "Amleto Monacelli has a short span. He certainly gets plenty of power on his shots," Baker says of the two-time Player of the Year.

GET A GRIP

As previously noted, altering your ball's surface with an abrasive or by adding polish adds to your flexibility. So, too, does the use of finger or thumb grips. These inserts are placed inside the holes of your ball.

Finger grips are usually fit fairly snugly and are designed to help your fingers remain in the ball longer before you release your shot. This increases the amount of time between the exit of your thumb and your fingers. The result is more revs and, with that, greater area and improved striking power.

Yellow finger grips are highly visible. As such, they can help you to see whether your ball is "revving up" or "rolling out."

Finger grips are made of either silicon or vinyl. The vinyl ones, according to Marc McDowell, allow you to stay in the ball longer than does silicon. He says vinyl produces a higher track and greater revs for added carrying power but at some sacrifice of control.

McDowell prefers the smoother release he enjoys with the silicon grips. Another factor is his desire to minimize the chance of injuring one of the bowler's most vulnerable body parts, his wrist. Because vinyl delays the release, in his opinion, it increases stress on the tendons.

The primary benefit of thumb inserts is that they provide a consistent feel to all of your balls. This is a big plus for the player who is likely to switch equipment as he or she bowls. Ours is a sport in which feel is vital. If your strike and spare ball don't feel the same, it will be harder for you to maintain a consistent release.

Why not just have your pro drill all of your balls the same way? You can and you should, but even if the size of the holes and the span are meant to be the same, they won't be identical. Thumb inserts come in specific sizes so

Finger grips (shown here outside the ball for illustration purposes) can help to get more lift into your release. (Photo by Steve Spatafore)

they help lessen the difference between Ball A and Ball B.

Benoit has overcome that problem, but with a price. He uses identical drilling specs for all his equipment. Unlike almost everyone else, he doesn't smooth the edges of the holes. That step, known as beveling, is done to protect the fingers and thumb.

Having "razor-sharp holes" forces Benoit to grip his ball gently. He thus avoids the tendency of some players to squeeze the ball, especially in pressure situations. Says Benoit, "If I were to grip too hard, I'd end up needing stitches."

His unique release, in which his hand and wrist are under the ball, is another factor that allows him to defy conventional ball-drilling wisdom.

GIVE CHEAP SHOES THE BOOT

Something else that can make a big difference is what you put on your feet. "You won't see Michael Jordan playing basketball in a $15 pair of sneakers," observes Baker. "Your shoes become very important once you get good at a sport."

Baker, who bowls right-handed, demands that his left foot be able to slide and that his right shoe provides maximum traction. Anything less and he can't use his leg power to full advantage. His preference runs toward a heavier-weight shoe that gives him outstanding support and lasts a long time. A more popular item among league players is the tennis-like variety of bowling shoes. They're lightweight and comfortable.

Either way, quality counts. Don't practice false economy when purchasing your shoes unless you're willing to buy another pair sooner than is necessary and to sacrifice your performance in the interim.

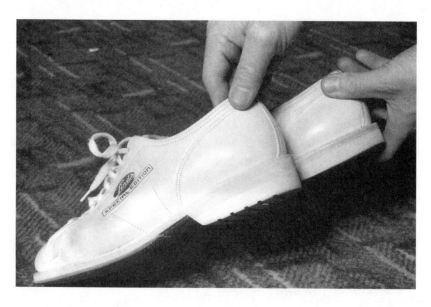

McDowell's shoes (note the built-up heel). (Photo by Steve Spatafore)

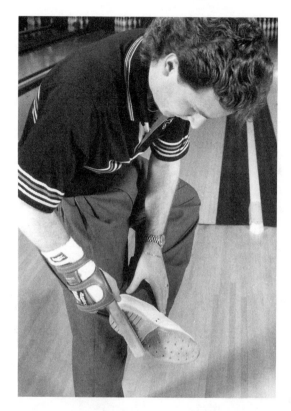

Always make certain that no foreign objects are attached to either shoe. (Photo by Steve Spatafore)

Also on the market are several wrist devices. They are designed to provide added support to help lock your wrist into the same position throughout your armswing. These are especially helpful to players who have weak forearms.

Having said that, we'll bet that you've seen some pros with very powerful forearms using a wrist device on television. There's a reason for that, and it has less to do with toppling pins than it does with basic economics. Our vocabulary word today, class, is "incentives."

There are two reasons why a pro selects a certain ball, shoe, wrist device, or shirt when bowling in a televised title round. The first reason is performance. The odds are very good that the ball is the one the player chose for the best chance of winning. But not always.

The factors that go into a decision when picking a shirt or deciding whether to wear a wrist device or a glove may have little to do with winning. Some pros, especially on the women's Tour, use wrist aids for added support. Many other players, particularly among the men, are more interested in their financial support.

Many companies offer incentive fees to bowlers who use their equipment on television because we consumers think that to "be like Mike" we have to drink the "right" thirst quencher. Should you believe that doing so makes you more likely to soar through the air, far be it from us to suggest otherwise.

However, if you are somewhat skeptical that your choice of a beverage has magical athletic implications, then may we suggest that you don't pay too much attention to whether your favorite pro is wearing a glove as he or she competes on the tube.

Buy a glove to protect your hand if needed, and purchase a wrist device if, in your opinion or on your pro's advice, it will help your release.

Some Touring pros have contracts with ball manufacturers. As of press time, Williams was affiliated with Ebonite, McDowell with Faball, and Benoit with Track. As such, they are contractually obligated to use their client's equipment exclusively in competition. While you can be certain they appreciate the added income, they wouldn't make such a commitment unless they had complete confidence in the quality of their company's equipment.

Despite the appeal of having a financial safety net, many top pros have not renewed their commercial arrangements when they found that the company with which they had aligned had fallen behind its rivals. As such, they are free to use whichever ball works best for them. Or, should they so decide, they can opt to use the ball whose company is paying the highest current bounty.

Benoit, who is affiliated with a major ball manufacturer, appreciates the importance of marrying the best equipment and the finest drilling techniques. (Photo by Steve Spatafore)

On virtually every TV show, free agent Baker selects the ball that he thinks gives him the best chance at winning. "The money I earn gets spent sooner than it should," he admits. "Winning a title lasts forever."

The rare exception might occur when he's pessimistic about his chances of success. "If I got lucky with one big game just to make the TV show as the final seed I might be tempted to take the extra $5,000 to throw the right ball. Let's face it, bowling isn't like other sports where you can

Although equipment plays a big role in Baker's success, he cautions against considering it a panacea. (Photo by Steve Spatafore)

get a million bucks for hitting .230 and then bitch about it."

There was a time when Baker was on the payroll of one of the major ball companies. His base salary was, in his words, "not exactly enough to thrill a Swiss banker." With performance incentives, he supplemented his income by approximately $25,000 during a good year.

That was a great arrangement for Baker because the company with which he was affiliated was considered at the time to have the best balls in the business. When that status changed as the other manufacturers caught up, Baker and many others reluctantly severed their alliances.

Unlike with shirts and wrist aids, Baker says, you can learn about what balls are hot by watching the Pro Bowlers Tour. States Baker: "A pro is going to throw whatever works. The balls that are working on the Tour usually work on anything."

A WORD FROM WILLIAMS

Conventional wisdom says that today's bowling balls are light-years ahead of their predecessors. Conventional wisdom, Williams suggests, might not be right.

Yes, scoring is definitely well up, but much of that can be attributed to urethane lane surfaces and less demanding oil patterns.

If the balls are so superior, Williams argues, then all of them would work well on all conditions. But they don't. One of the real keys on the pro Tours is discovering which is the optimum ball with the best weight combination to match the player's roll on that condition. A thorough understanding of such factors is one reason that many star veterans have a huge advantage over both their less-knowledgeable rivals and over Tour newcomers.

Because there is no inherent edge in merely owning a urethane ball, it's vital that you buy the ball that's most effective for your game on the conditions on which you

In addition to being a world-class bowler, Walter Ray is a five-time world horseshoe-pitching champion.

normally compete. The importance of making the right decision is just one more reason why the expertise of your pro is so essential.

It's not enough that the person with whom you do business be knowledgeable. Trust is also required. Pro shop operators are as human as the rest of us. Some of them may be inclined to encourage customers to purchase the equipment that either yields the highest margin of profit, is most prevalent in their inventory, or happens to be the one that works best for that pro's personal game.

When 10 different customers ended up buying from the same line of balls, the odds are that the pro might be more interested in his or her needs than in yours.

If you can find that happy combination of the right pro to drill the right ball in the right way for your needs, the results should be noticeable. In bowling, having the right equipment is half the battle. Now it's up to you to learn how to use it to full advantage. It's time for some serious talk about lane conditions.

4

LANE CONDITIONS

As any sociologist who bowls can tell you, we are all products of our environment. Mark Baker grew up rolling at Champion Lanes, which had long and thick oil without any swing area. "It was," he laughs, "45 feet of sauce." Early on, Baker honed the skills necessary to play a deep inside line.

Bob Benoit spent most of his developmental years competing on the lacquer lanes of Rose Bowl West in Wichita, Kansas. Few centers have ever had as pronounced a track area. "There was literally a dark area between the 12th and the 18th boards where almost everybody rolled their strike shots," Benoit recalls. "If your ball got out to the 10th board, there was no way it would get back to the headpin."

Benoit became an accuracy-oriented player who threw the ball much straighter than Baker. Given the facilities in

The three basic routes to the pocket: Baker is deep inside, McDowell uses the track, and Williams plays the gutter. (Photo by Steve Spatafore)

which they learned to bowl, it's little wonder that Baker and Benoit developed dissimilar styles.

Not until Benoit took his sabbatical to "learn how to bowl all over again" could he produce a sufficiently powerful roll to be able to compete successfully on the national Tour. The need for accuracy that he learned at Rose Bowl West gives him a big edge over the many players who have power but can't consistently hit their target.

To this day, Baker prefers to play deep inside. That means that he stands on the left side of the lane and aims his ball toward the right channel. At some point his shot will grip the lane and change its trajectory so that it hooks into the pocket. This technique is also known as "bellying" the ball.

Had Benoit not revised his style, his straight shot would do best at a house (like Rose Bowl West) with a pronounced track area. He'd also fare well when the condition called for "playing up the boards." That's accomplished by standing well to the right of the center of the approach and aiming the ball straight ahead. Aim toward the pocket and you're "pointing it up." Stand all the way right and you're "playing the gutter." In all of these cases, your target is either the same- or a higher-numbered board than the one from which you release your shot.

Sounds complicated? With experience and practice, you can become versatile enough to fare well playing either inside or outside. The odds are very strong that one of the two techniques comes more easily to you.

Even on the pro Tours, players often refer to their "A game." That's when they can play their favorite shot because the lane conditions favor what they do best. Although the better pros can play anywhere on the lane, they, too, tend to have a zone that they strongly prefer.

Since 1981 the PBA National Championship has been contested at Ducat's Imperial Lanes in Toledo, Ohio. Not until the later half of the 1980s did that center change from lacquer-based to urethane surface lanes. Until then, notes Williams: "It had a pronounced track area. It was very tough on many of the younger players who tend to cross more boards. In that house at that time to consistently strike you had to keep your shot in a narrow path to the pocket."

Unlike the pros, you probably won't be faced with a wide range of conditions. The house in which you bowl will probably be oiled in the same way by the same person at the same time on the same days throughout the year. Unless you travel from center to center to compete in tournaments or several leagues, you won't require the Williams-like versatility that is the hallmark of the great player.

One quality that separates the pros from the rest of us is their ability to adapt. The stars on the LPBT and PBA who have stood the test of time do so because they're able to make the physical and strategic adjustments to score on a variety of conditions.

These athletes have shown the ability to change speeds and hand positions. They can play well while using all types of strike lines. They are capable of adjusting their hand or wrist positions to alter both the amount of hook and the break point (the distance down the lane when the ball's trajectory begins to curve toward the pocket).

Being versatile is one way that first-rate players demonstrate just how demanding it is to become a great bowler. One can always reach for a different ball to help adjust to lane conditions. While that shortcut (and the incredible amounts of knowledge and experience needed to exploit it) is very important in the modern game, it's not a cure-all.

Having a wide range of shots allows a bowler to adapt from week to week, day to day, block to block, game to game, and even frame to frame.

According to many pros, the condition for the televised title round is often different from what had existed up to that time in that particular tournament. "What you see when you're bowling on TV is a fresh oil pattern," observes Williams. "Usually, you don't want to play deep inside on fresh oil."

The bowler whose "A game" is to stand left of center on the approach must often either move his feet or make an adjustment with equipment, his release, ball speed, or a combination of the above.

With rare exception, to achieve Bowler of the Year honors a player not only must excel at his or her "A game," but must also be very formidable when employing a back-up style. The top performer of 1980, Wayne Webb, was credited by Baker for possessing such a range of qualities.

Offers Baker: "The biggest difference between the better pros and amateurs is that we can play the entire lane and we can read our own ball faster. Wayne was the best at that. I've seen him roll a 270 one game and start with a double on a new pair of lanes in the next game only to change balls. Even without having missed, he could tell that his shot didn't have the optimum reaction. Then he'd shoot another 270 using the new ball or a different line."

A critical factor in tournament play is how one performs in the first frame after changing lanes. If you hit your target and can feel yourself executing correctly, you will immediately discover if the new pair is similar to the lanes you just left.

What makes that so important is that getting an accurate reading allows the versatile player to make an immediate adjustment. On Tour, making good decisions is but half of the battle. Winning the war requires making good decisions a frame (or a few) before your opponent does. Being first provides a huge competitive advantage.

If Williams had his druthers, oil patterns would be such that he could always stand just inside the right chan-

Although he prefers to stand farther to the right, Williams's greatness owes to being able to excel from many angles. (Photo by Steve Spatafore)

nel while rolling his ball hard and relatively straight. A slight hook at the back end would give his shot an optimum entry angle into the pocket to maximize his carry.

The key to Williams's success has been that while it isn't his preference to play a deep inside line, he is sufficiently versatile to be competitive while doing so. Although he has yet to win a tournament when conditions force him to move considerably to the left on the approach, he has used that line to qualify for match play and title rounds on numerous occasions.

That range of talent distinguishes players like Baker and Williams from run-of-the-mill pros. There are those who have enjoyed a hot streak only to fade into oblivion when conditions change. Like the dinosaur, they risk extinction because they can't modify their games to suit a changing environment.

Top pros, like Texan Del Ballard, Jr., give the amateurs an annual reality check at the U.S. Open. (Photo courtesy of the PBA)

These types are referred to in Tour parlance as "condition champions." While they're sufficiently gifted to be able to dominate while playing their "A games," they are like fish out of water in other situations. They are soon "sent home" to work on their games. Only a handful, such as Benoit, have the skill and the will to prevail.

The task is made even more challenging by being unable to "road test" their game at home after having implemented the changes. Rolling on house conditions while preparing to compete on the PBA Tour is like readying yourself to swim the English Channel by training in a kiddie pool.

How different are house from Tour conditions? The highest average in any year on the PBA Tour is likely to be in the 215–220 range. Hundreds, perhaps thousands, of amateurs finish the season with a higher mean.

Comparing the two is as unfair as having a race in which one contestant sprints on the track while the other must run in sand. An interesting phenomenon occurs annually at the U.S. Open. The 96 amateurs in the 240-player field get a reality check when they're forced to compete on the most demanding oil pattern in bowling.

The typical U.S. Open sees at least a 15-pin differential in the composite averages of the pros compared to those of the BPAA (Bowling Proprietors Association of America) entries. Only once since 1983 has an amateur finished among the top 10 (Jeff Mackey and Bill Ryan, Jr., placed sixth and seventh in 1987).

John Eiss won the distinction of being 1992's leading amateur by finishing 24th. His 205.7 average for 56 games was 19.5 pins lower than that of qualifying leader Scott Devers.

Bowling's minor leagues, the series of regional tournaments that the PBA sanctions, are almost always rolled on house conditions. Scores tend to be astronomical, with winners usually determined by their ability to carry.

There are many wanna-be types who excel against star pros on the regional level but who can't compete on the Tour when they have to execute more precise shots merely to hit the pocket.

Even the occasional house condition that's relatively difficult is unlikely to vary as much or be nearly as demanding as those found on the Tour. Unless you plan on taking your ball on the road, there is little need to attempt to become versatile.

If your goal is to do well as an amateur in your area (including shooting that elusive 300), you'll probably be just fine if you concentrate all of your energies on developing and maximizing your "A game."

The size of your ambitions dictates whether it's necessary for you to go beyond doing only what you do best. If your "A game" suits the house conditions on which you bowl exclusively, there is little need to learn how to do anything else. Be forewarned that you may suffer when the conditions at your favorite house invariably change or if you decide to bowl somewhere else.

Before you can become versatile, it's important that you can do one thing well. The first step is to concentrate your energies on learning how to "repeat." Obtaining a consistency of motions throughout your delivery is essential. That's one quality that all good bowlers share.

Even though we appreciate your patronage, nobody will add pins to your score because the style of your delivery goes "by the book." An unorthodox player can beat a stylist by consistently duplicating his or her movements.

Once that's accomplished, learning how to have a back-up plan of attack can be a godsend to the bowler who competes on a wide variety of conditions.

Either way, the first step for all players is to have a solid "A game." The odds are that you won't bowl a 300 or even post a respectable average until you can do one thing very well. Don't worry about learning how to play a wide variety of strike lines or how to change ball speed, wrist position, or your release until you are confident that your "A game" is strong.

True versatility means being good at a lot of things while being great when conditions favor your game. To become mediocre on all conditions is hardly a worthwhile ambition.

Decide your goal for yourself. Are you aiming to be a "condition champion," or do you demand more? If you think that versatility is a missing link in your game, you'll have to learn how to make physical adjustments (by changing ball speed as well as hand or wrist positions) and how to change your game plan (elements of strategy include knowing how to bowl on all parts of the lane and changing balls).

DISCOVERING THE OIL LINE

Baker's background was at a center where any navigational errors had better be to the left. Miss his target by two boards to the right, and his ball wouldn't even touch the headpin. But when he was two boards off line to the left, his shot rarely strayed into the nose. As a result, his slightly high hit rewarded him with either a strike (thanks to tripping the 4 pin) or a good count with a relatively easy spare conversion.

Nowadays, Baker tries to find the "oil line" on a lane. That's the route to the pocket in which his shot will hold the line if he's missed his target to the left. The secret is to have the drier boards to the right of the ball (to allow it to hook back) and oilier ones to its left (to retard the hook as the ball begins to stray toward the nose or Brooklyn side).

Having what's known as a "hold area" helps Baker to

relax. "When I have hold, I become looser. When I'm looser I throw the ball much better," Baker says.

Amplifies Williams: "There are times when I feel that I can't miss. At other times, I feel like I have to execute a near-perfect delivery just to get to the pocket."

The sense of having some room for error often provides a big confidence boost which, in turn, can make a bowler less error-prone. In the classic chicken-and-egg case, the correlation between confidence and margin for error is unmistakable.

Part of that comes from ability. An even bigger part is being on a lane condition that suits your "A game" coupled with knowing how to play the lane. All of the great players on the PBA Tour can strike from any angle on any lane using any ball. But as talented as they may be, none of them is going to produce a perfect delivery on every shot. By discovering the combination of the optimum line, ball type, speed, and release, they greatly increase their odds of striking on a less-than-ideal delivery.

The sense of having some room for error often provides a big confidence boost which, in turn, can make a bowler less error-prone.

The art of playing a lane becomes more important as you progress in the sport. The better the level of competition, the greater the significance of your claiming every possible strike.

As for rolling a 300, it may be even more important for you to be playing the lane correctly than it is for a pro. That's because over a given period of time, the pro may roll enough outstanding shots that he or she won't require as much area as you or I. As for us amateurs, we had better find the strike line that is the most forgiving because we aren't nearly as likely to produce 12 consecutive great shots.

Before we progress, a few words about lane conditioner (also known as oil) are required. As a lubricant that protects the lane, oil minimizes the amount of friction imparted to the ball. Not only does this preserve the lane, it also affects your shot. Less friction means less gripping action. A ball sliding through oil usually reacts much like a bald tire skidding on an icy road.

Normally, the back end isn't oiled. That means that the bowling ball and the lane surface are in direct contact. A higher coefficient of friction results.

The condition of a wet front section of a lane and a dry back end is why you see the pros' shots roll relatively straight until they suddenly veer at a sharp angle toward the pocket. This late hooking action is a combination of friction's effects and the bowler's powerful release.

The shot of a typical pro "revs up" as it nears the pins. Williams, our resident physics expert, defines that as an increase in angular velocity. In laymen's English, the number of revolutions per time unit has increased as the shot approached the pins. A typical Baker shot will have 15–18 revolutions during its 60-foot journey, of which the majority occur during the last 20 feet.

Revs, in and of themselves, are but a part of the equation. Nobody gets more revs than a three-year-old who pushes the ball while on his or her knees. But the youngster's shots are rolled slowly (and with a lighter ball) and aren't angled toward the pocket so that massive deflection by the pins is unavoidable.

Revs, when combined with an optimum ball speed, are required to get the job done right.

CARRYDOWN

As a liquid, oil is transient. The rolling of bowling balls over a lane causes the conditioner to move and the condition to change. As the ball travels toward the pins, it removes some oil from the heads (the front part of the lane). Portions of that oil are deposited on the drier segment of the lane (the back end), while some remains on the ball.

The movement of oil from the heads to the back end is known as "carrydown." As that occurs, the front of the lane has less oil. When that happens, it's referred to as having "broken down."

Because of the oil's transience, your ball will react differently. The changes are subtle and are usually noticeable only over a period of several frames, or even games.

The first transition that a newly oiled lane experiences after some usage is for the lane to become "tighter" (less back-end hook). Next, the ball begins to hook sooner but may not finish as strongly as you would like. Finally, the ball hooks so excessively that it becomes difficult to maintain accuracy.

The worst stage of the transition from a newly oiled condition to a dry lane occurs when your shots are more likely to hook early (which isn't normally desired by most players) and not to hook as much as they near the pins (even less desirable).

If you bowled for several hours, you might experience the entire range of conditions. The chances are that over the course of three games of league play, you will only be subjected to more modest transitions. It's important to note that the majority of league players aren't rolling immediately after the back ends were cleaned. By the time you've arrived for an evening session, much of the carrydown has already taken place.

Throughout these changing phases, the difference in ball reaction dictates that you make adjustments. To do so very well requires both knowledge and physical ability.

When the lane starts to tighten, you can change your line slightly (Williams likes to move to the right). You can change equipment (perhaps a softer-shell ball will help).

You can change your release to get more power. Or you can keep throwing the ball just as you did at the start of your night and wonder why you aren't getting the same results.

Like the dinosaur, you must adapt or face the consequences.

On the Tour, the lanes are oiled every morning. At the start, the head area is wet, and the back ends are dry. This tends to favor the straight-shot players.

In contrast, the night block tests the players' abilities to compete after carrydown occurs. Bowlers who tend to do better on that condition are the power-oriented (big hook) types. Because the PBA format alters a player's starting time from day to day, to be a dominant force requires the ability to excel on both extremes.

As to you, the league player, the odds are that your center has a consistent schedule of when and how it maintains its lanes. You need to discover if you're rolling on a "fresh" condition or if several leagues have used the facility since it was last oiled.

Doing so allows you to handpick the bowling time that's best for your game. If you are the Williams-type, you will probably prefer to bowl just after the lanes have been oiled. Those from the Mark Baker school like to roll later at night. They would find it even more advantageous to bowl on the second day after lane conditioner was applied.

Here's Williams's strategy for adapting to carrydown: "Typically on Tour you'll see bowlers using a harder-shell ball during the first few games of a morning block. Every two to three frames, I move my feet one board to the right. The softer-shell balls are preferred at night. If I have a light hit as the result of a lot of carrydown, I'm more likely to make a two-and-one move to the right." This refers to moving one's feet two boards and one's target a single board in the same direction.

Bowl long enough, and the back-end oil will become

depleted. At this point the heads have long since been broken down. It's time to move left or find a ball that is designed for use on a dry lane (a left-handed player moves to the right).

ENTRY ANGLE

The angle at which your shot enters the pocket is a key factor in determining its effect. A straight ball is likely to deflect to the right after hitting the headpin. Excessive deflection is poison.

That would seem to indicate that zero percent deflection would represent the ideal, but bowling's principles aren't so easily defined.

Lack of deflection is almost as undesirable as excessive deflection. The ball that slices through the pins like a knife through butter is a recent phenomenon. "Urethane splits" and "urethane taps" often result. Many a great shot has been marred by a stubborn 8 pin that resulted when the ball drove the 5 pin directly backward rather than into the 8 pin. Possible splits are the 4-9 (the 6-8 for southpaws) or the rarer 7-9 (8-10).

The light hit that enters the pocket at a steep angle is likely to leave the 2-10 split or even something as ugly as the 2-4-6-7-10 combination.

So if no deflection and excessive deflection are the enemies, just how much deflection is desirable and why? We're glad that you asked.

Assuming you hook your shots (or throw a straight ball angled in from the channel toward the pocket), there are some things that you want to occur to get that "X" consistently.

1. Hit your target.

A shot moving from right to left (for the right-handed player) should impact between the headpin and the 3 pin.

Left-handed bowlers aim for the 1-2 pocket. Those who roll a back-up ball (also known as a "reverse curve") reverse the formula.

2. Generate adequate (but not too much) power.

Here's where ball deflection comes into play. On a "perfect" strike, your ball makes direct contact with only four pins (the 1-3-5-9 for a right-handed player and the 1-2-5-8 for a southpaw).

The strike ball of 1991 Player of the Year David Ozio actually only impacts directly with four pins. (Photo courtesy of the PBA)

After a right-handed player's shot hits the pocket, the headpin sails to the left. It sets off a chain reaction to topple the 2, 4, and 7 pins. The 3 pin takes care of the 6 and the 10 pins. The ball deflects slightly to the right. It then hits the right side of the 5 pin so that the 5 takes out the 8 pin as the ball removes the 9 pin.

The southpaw's shot sends the 5 pin into the 9 pin while the ball hits the 8 pin.

Excessive deflection results in corner-pin leaves and includes several forms of pocket splits. As noted, inadequate deflection, while not usually as costly, can leave you with a tap or a split.

3. Be consistent.

The amount that your shot hooks depends on many factors. All of these variables are affected by your hand the less your ball will hook). You don't have to do everything by the book, but being consistent in your movements is key. Bowling is a game of repetition. The more unorthodox your style, the more important it is to be able to repeat.

These three principles—accuracy, power, and consistency—are the keys to rolling that 300. That doesn't mean that you must produce 12 consecutive flawless deliveries to obtain that many picture-perfect strikes. In fact, there are other varieties of strikes than the aforementioned "traditional" type.

The "wall shot" is a light hit in which your power causes the headpin to topple the 2 pin into the 8 pin. The headpin then ricochets off of the sidewall (the left segment of the lane for a right-handed bowler and vice versa) and rebounds into play to help eliminate the 4, 5, and 7 pins (a lefty equivalent tackles the 5, 6, and 10 pins).

Another variety is the "swishing" strike (also known

as "ripping the rack" or a "rip rack"). On a hit that is only a bit light, the ball sends the 5 pin sliding to the far corner of the deck to remove the 7 pin (for a righty) or the 10 pin (for a lefty). To produce either the swishing hit or the wall shot is only partially a function of good luck.

Your ability to carry these types of hits involves more than just your line (a benefit of using an outside line is obtaining better carry on half-hits) or imparting an efficient roll. This is another instance in which the characteristics of the center in which you bowl play a big role. Places with lively sidewalls are far more conducive to better scoring.

The difference between carrying a less-than-optimum shot and being faced with a split is often slight. The ultimate pitfall is suffering the "rip 7-10," in which the headpin slides either in front of or behind the 7 pin (the 10 pin for a lefty) while also leaving the equivalent of a weak 10 (lefty: weak 7).

It isn't merely fortuitous when the right-handed Player A carries a wall-shot strike or only leaves the 2 pin, while the shot of Bowler B leaves the 2-4-5 or the bucket (2-4-5-8). The difference is that Player A rolls the ball with sufficient power to make the headpin fly back into play, while Player B's shot is so weak that the headpin slides harmlessly into the far channel.

Ball speed is also a factor. Shots that are too fast send pins skyward rather than into other sticks. Shots that are too slow don't take maximum advantage of lively sidewalls. Discovering the happy medium for your roll is a big help.

The "trip 4" occurs on a high hit. The 2 pin flies in front of the 4 pin but returns to play after hitting the sidewall to eliminate the 4 pin (and sometimes the 7 pin as well). The mirror image is the "trip 6" for the left-handed player (thanks to help from the 3 pin).

Baker says that having a hold area is more important than having added swing. (Photo by Steve Spatafore)

That Mark Baker is more concerned with having a hold area (to the left) than he is about having a swing area (to the right) speaks of bowling's odds. There are far more ways that you can get a strike on a light hit than on the high variety. Because of that, most bowlers are more concerned about avoiding the high hit than they are with averting a light one.

Either way, entry angle is important. A hook that is too pronounced is said to come into the pocket "behind" the headpin. While that analysis is an exaggeration, it is true that the steep angle can result in leaving the 10 pin.

The "solid" 10 pin leave (7 pin for a left-handed

player) results when there is slightly too much deflection on an otherwise well-executed delivery.

As a result, the 6 pin sails around the belly (or the neck) of the 10 pin (lefty equivalent: the 4 pin missing the 7 pin). The "soft" 10 pin is more worrisome. The 6 pin is pushed into the channel. This results when there is significantly more ball deflection than on the "solid" leave.

A "solid" 10 pin (or 7 pin) is something of an occupational hazard. Pros make very slight adjustments in ball speed (slower) or their line (feet one board in the direction of your bowling hand) or where they stand on the approach (a few inches farther from the foul line at the start of the delivery).

Unless you are a very gifted player who is well-practiced, we don't recommend adjusting after leaving a "solid" corner pin. Overall, you've made a good shot. If you can repeat that consistently, you will get more than your share of strikes.

However, the "soft" corner pin is a warning sign. If you hit your target and executed a good delivery, it might mean that the lane has changed. If so, make a carrydown adjustment (a slightly softer ball, slower ball speed, or move one board on the approach, right-handed bowlers to the right or left-handed players to the left).

There's an axiom that you only make an adjustment after a good shot. If the "soft" leave was caused by missing your target or a faulty release, there is no reason to do anything different on your subsequent delivery beyond improving your execution.

Too Much Power?

The ball that roars into the pocket from a great angle can carry a lot of half-hits, but it also leaves more than its share of taps. There is a happy medium.

Remember the tradeoff between accuracy and power.

The more of one you strive for, the less of the other you are likely to obtain.

A moderate hook is best for most players. It gives you more power than the straight shooters and greater accuracy than the crankers. If you look at the qualities of the PBA stars who enjoyed long and productive careers, you will find that almost all of them rolled shots that were accurate and featured outstanding carrying power.

Inaccuracy must be averted. When your ball smacks against the nose of the headpin, you will likely be faced with one of the following headaches: the 7-10, 4-6, 4-6-7-10, 4-6-7, 6-7-10, 4-6-7-9-10, or 4-6-7-8-10.

PLAYING THE TRACK

As opposed to playing at the track, picking the right "horse" in this case means ignoring Robert Frost's poetic advice by choosing the route that is the most traveled. Bowling's track area is the well-worn path on the lane between the foul line and the pocket.

Let's say that the lanes were oiled in the afternoon, and you're scheduled to roll at 9 o'clock in the evening league. If you arrive early, you might note that seven of the ten bowlers in the earlier league are using a similar strike line.

Logic dictates that there will be more oil to either side of that path than there is in that route. It's as if they've "carved" a zone that, like a good surfer's wave, will carry you happily to the shore.

Track areas were more common in the old days. The lacquer finishes often left a track that was discernable to the naked eye. While that isn't nearly as common in this era of urethane-finished lanes (some of which are made of a synthetic wood substitute), there can still be a track-like zone that you can exploit. It is certainly to your advantage to bowl in a late league that follows a league of high-average players.

Williams refers to that phenomenon as a "natural wall." In his opinion, it's often "a better shot than was put down by the center in the first place. Players who hook the ball can take better advantage. Instead of having a path to the lane that's 20-feet long from the original oil pattern, it could be 35 to 40 feet. It's a longer route for the ball to be guided into the pocket."

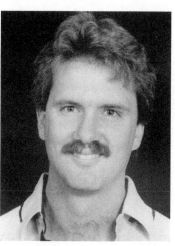

If you really want to see this man smile, have Williams bowl on a "natural wall." (Photo courtesy of the PBA)

As with many athletic axioms, this one doesn't hold 100 percent of the time. Adds Williams: "The big hook bowlers love to play on the shift following a scratch league. However, if the lanes didn't get enough oil to start with, by the time that second shift bowls they will be dry and the lanes will be hooking like crazy."

Assuming that's not the case where you bowl, that second shift can increase your chances at bagging a 300. To find the "natural wall" will require some trial and error.

A good place to begin, offers Benoit, is "between the second and the third arrows. That's where you'll find the track in most centers. In recent years with short oil patterns, it's moved a little bit farther to the outside."

Because there are many more right-handed bowlers than there are southpaws, this method isn't as applicable for lefties. The lane gets worn down more often and quicker on the right side. It is therefore more important for a right-handed player to know where the track is located and be able to exploit the situation when a pronounced track exists.

OBSERVING AND COPYING OTHERS

Good bowlers are "scouts." The pros make it a point to notice where and how a tournament's leaders are playing the lanes. There are scores of stories of players who were at the bottom of the standings in an event until they noticed that a fellow competitor with a style similar to their own was using a very different strategy to great success. Imitation is not only the sincerest form of flattery, it can be a great scoring weapon.

If you are a higher-average type who bowls with other serious players, the odds are good that at least a few players in your league have qualities much like your own. If you are struggling, why not glance at them as they bowl to discover if they are employing tactics that you might put to good use?

Benoit keeps an eye on Don Genalo. Known as a down-and-in player, Genalo "likes to play the oil line," according to Benoit. Even though their games aren't that similar, Benoit gains vital information by observing Genalo's strategy.

Even watching a player whose style is miles removed from your own can provide clues. Williams's game is certainly closer to that of Dave Ferraro's than of ultra-power player Kelly Coffman. "But," notes Williams, "if Kelly is striking and Dave isn't, I'll watch to see what Kelly is doing and I'll know not to play where Dave is on the lane."

LANE GEOGRAPHY

There's a tongue-in-cheek bumper sticker that declares that good girls go to heaven but bad girls go everywhere. In bowling, good players hit the pocket. Great ones can consistently carry their hits from everywhere.

The requirements for playing the gutter are very different from those when bellying a shot from a deep inside line. Among the adjustments one can make are in release, ball speed, and equipment.

The farther Benoit moves inside, the slower his ball speed. (Photo by Steve Spatafore)

Here's a quick chart to help you on your way:

Outside Line	**Inside Line**
Ball speed More	**Ball speed** Slower
Target Around the first arrow	**Target** From the second to the fourth (center) arrow
Ball Harder shell (Pros often use a three-piece construction when playing this angle)	**Ball** Probably a softer shell (for greater hooking and gripping power) combined with a two-piece construction to maximize carry
Priority Accuracy is more important than power	**Priority** Power is more important than accuracy
Advantage Easier to carry half-hits, especially for players whose shots don't normally generate great numbers of revolutions	**Advantage** Better line to play on a very dry lane

If the talk of two- and three-piece balls is daunting, don't despair. Just refer back to the last chapter. As to what steps you can take to become more proficient at playing a different part of the lane from your "A game," see our practice pointers in Chapter 5.

For specific advice on the two strategies, we turn to the man who has shown he can do both. When playing inside, Williams says that he "slows my speed down and I try to get more side roll."

Although he's won title-round berths using that line, he acknowledges that "it's tough for me to play that shot on either heavily oiled or newly oiled lanes. I need for the track to break down so as to create that belly swing. I can play that on fresh back ends. I can play it after the track

breaks down and there is oil to the left (of the strike line).
I need a lot of area to loop the ball because, with that line,
I'm less accurate."

The good news, at least on house conditions, is that
Williams has discovered that "the outside part of the lane
tends to hook more than the inside. That's especially true
for right-handed players."

SYNTHETIC LANES

Just as artificial turf changes the way baseball is played,
so do synthetic lanes affect bowling. The wood-substitute
surfaces figure to gain in prevalence given that manufacturers promote them to bowling-center proprietors as offering longer life spans.

According to Baker, synthetic lanes are "either dead
walled or dead impossible." This feast-or-famine syn-
drome means that you stand a better chance of bagging a
300 on the newfangled variety of lane. You're also more
vulnerable to suffering through some 130s.

Although they don't know of any scientific research to
prove their sentiments, all four pros agree that a friendly
synthetic pair provides the sport's best scoring environment. Williams cites several PBA records that have been
set on them, including many of his own.

Certain styles of players and ball rolls tend to thrive
on synthetics. Del Ballard, Jr., excels on them. Benoit cites
Ballard's "heavy-rolling ball" and slower speed as key
factors.

There are two words of caution. Notes Benoit, "Synthetics break down far more and far quicker than a wood
lane." As such, he makes a line adjustment at the first sign
of even a modestly high hit. "As soon as I leave a four-pin,
I'm moving," he asserts.

Another danger is the approach. The same lane can

have both slippery and sticky spots. Test the area around the foul line before rolling your first practice ball. Doing so will help you to avoid either a needlessly missed shot or, even worse, an injury.

MAKING ADJUSTMENTS

Not moving enough to compensate for lane conditions is a big problem among many of the better amateur bowlers who ought to know better. So says Bob Benoit, who suggests: "Don't inch over. Move over! You're not being competitive if you take nine frames to get lined up. I'd rather make a big move early in the game and suffer the consequences of one split than wait too long or be too timid."

Continues Benoit: "The pocket is located 17½ boards in from the channel. If I leave the bucket (2-4-5-8), it's because my ball reached the pins at about the 14th board. That means I'm three-and-a-half boards light." If he has hit his target and executed what he felt was a good release, Bob will move his feet "two to three boards to the right" on his next shot on that lane.

As always, a determination regarding both the amount and the pattern of the oil dictates your strategy. If the conditioner is liberally applied for the majority of the lane (in bowling parlance, "heavy" and "long"), Benoit wants to get his ball rolling more. To do so, he stays behind the ball and only allows his hand to rotate minimally. To make the ball skid farther on a dry lane, he rotates his hand counterclockwise (lefties: clockwise) during his shot and begins his delivery with his hand more on the side of the ball rather than behind it.

If the oil is sparse and isn't applied far down the lane ("light" and "short"), he'll use more of a suitcase grip. Benoit holds the ball as he would the handle of a suitcase, locking his fingers into a position about 3 o'clock (left-handed bowlers keep theirs at 9 o'clock).

A slight adjustment in hand position from Benoit's normal behind-the-ball technique (left) to the suitcase grip (right) dramatically changes his shot's hooking pattern. (Photo by Steve Spatafore)

There are other adjustments that are less complicated
to make. For example, a hooking lane can be overcome by
using an aiming point beyond the arrows to help delay
your shot's break point. Benoit eyes the splice that goes
across the lane (at the 16-foot point, where the pine meets
the heads). Why target past the arrows?

Benoit has noticed a personal tendency to throw his
shots too slowly when his target is close. He uses that
knowledge to make adjustments in shot velocity. When he
wants to roll shots slower, he uses an arrow as his target.

There are times when one can test a shot. The best of
these opportunities occurs during the warm-up period
prior to the start of the competition. After you have found
the line that seems to be working, you may wish to experiment to see if there is an even better strategy.

The fill ball in the 10th frame of a game whose outcome has already been decided provides an opportunity to
apply trial and error to your educated guess as to a different line, speed, ball, release, or any combination of the
above.

A somewhat more risky proposition is to forgo trying
to "save the wood" on an "impossible" split (such as the 7-
10, 7-9, 8-10, or the 4-6) in favor of throwing a strike ball
to test your alternate strategy. Keep in mind that doing so
following a strike in the previous frame means you'll be
losing two pins on the scoresheet for every one stick that
you fail to knock over on your split shot.

To Each His Own

Even for the pros, there is a wide divergence in the types
of adjustments preferred. Some players make almost all of
their changes by switching equipment. Others move on the
lane. A third group alters parts of the delivery.

The most basic rule is to move your feet in the same
direction as you missed. In other words, if your shot went

too far to the left, move your feet to the left (but use the same target on the lane). If you missed to the right, move to the right.

A ball that is one or two boards off line requires a one-board move. A shot that misses by three to five boards calls for a two- or a three-board adjustment. Like all rules, you may need to modify the above advice based on your experience. Trial and error, coupled with acute observation, yields the "secrets" of playing a lane.

Not everyone prefers to change his or her strike line. McDowell says that he's more comfortable changing the speed of his shots. "Maybe it's because of my legs," offers the former placekicker. "I can come to the line a little faster or slower to naturally change my ball speed. If there is a lot of oil, I'll shorten my approach, which will make my shot go slower. If the lane is more dry, I'll lengthen my approach so my shot is faster.

One reason that works is because McDowell's athleticism lends itself to inherently good timing. For the amateur who isn't as gifted or who hardly practices, such a change could throw his or her delivery out of kilter.

Many of us are more inclined to alter the wrist position. The more one "cups" the wrist, the greater the hook. A wrist that is bent backward retards hook.

McDowell, despite his great ability, says that he isn't as comfortable tinkering with that aspect of his delivery. "If I really cup the ball, my armswing tends to get out of whack," he acknowledges. "I try to keep that part of my game consistent."

It all comes down to becoming sufficiently aware of your own assets and liabilities so as to determine which type of adjustment is more naturally suited to your game. Discovering that can take years. Cautions McDowell: "Don't try to do what you aren't capable of doing. The key is to always stay within your own game."

Failure to do so is a big cause of the downfall of many

One adjustment McDowell never makes is to tinker with his wrist position. (Photo by Steve Spatafore)

players on many levels, including the pros. Like many sports, bowling is susceptible to trends. There have been periods of time when the "straight" players have dominated and other times in which the power players have been in the driver's seat.

Given that one's income is directly linked to performance, it's very tempting for a player to alter his game drastically when conditions aren't in his favor. The danger is that one is rarely successful doing what doesn't come naturally. And, when the trend is reversed back into one's favor, the player may have messed up his or her game and may not be competitive.

A better option, as proven by McDowell in 1992, is to

become sharper at what you do best. In that year, his best as a pro, McDowell won three titles and paced the PBA in earnings with $176,215. Aside from his success and that of Dave Ferraro, from the right side of the lane that was a year that belonged to power players.

"Yeah, I saw the crankers throwing a lot of strikes," McDowell says. "I saw how Bob Vespi was able to open up a lane. But I knew that I don't have his release to be able to do that. There is just no way that I can keep up by playing that way with a player who does that naturally. If I tried to play Vespi's game, he'd pound me into the ground.

"During the weeks when the power players dominated, I refused to get discouraged. I'd grind out a paycheck so that when the turn came for the straight players, I could take advantage. I knew that most weeks there would be at least a reasonable shot out there for the straight guys, too. I proved that and so did Dave (Ferraro)."

Not everyone was as patient. Among those who temporarily fell by the wayside was 1991 Player of the Year David Ozio. After a slow start following his career year, Ozio made major changes in his game that, in McDowell's opinion, proved detrimental.

"David Ozio is a great bowler, but it was as if he was looking to fix problems that didn't really exist," observes McDowell. "David doesn't have the roll to play the ultra-power game. Unless you have a Vespi-like release, it won't do you any good to try to bowl like him."

That doesn't mean that moderate changes in one's game won't pay dividends. Williams ranks among the Tour's best at being able to compete with either a relatively straight ball or a substantial hook. However, he never "cranks it up" in an attempt to match the ultra-power players board for board.

Also ranking high on the versatility scale are Norm Duke and Pete Weber.

ROLL YOUR
"A GAME" WHENEVER POSSIBLE

Except for that very rare lucky day when everything seems to go your way, to really string strikes you had better be playing your "A game" on your "A line" with your favorite ball to bag a 300.

There may be times when the lane conditions make it almost impossible to do so. As golfers know, you can only take what the course gives to you. There will be days when you measure success by lower standards. When the oil pattern isn't to your liking, your ability to grind out a respectable score is key.

There is a great rule of thumb regarding how you should react to the environment: The lower the scores, the fewer boards your shot should cross. When the lanes are at their toughest, you will gain a competitive edge by keeping your shots in play. More than one pro has moved to his or her right (southpaws to the left) and proceeded to throw "a rocket to the pocket."

Happily, because you're refining your abilities for a more stable environment, the odds are that the majority of outings will see you striving for big numbers.

On those occasions, here's a clue as to what strategy might best suit your needs. States Williams: "Power players get more of their perfect games when playing left of the 12th or 13th board. Straight players tend to get more when playing right of 12 or 13."

Either way, the bottom line is that by being both knowledgeable and able to repeat, you will greatly increase your chances of producing a 300 game. "You have to know how to play the lane," cautions Williams. "A pair can be walled, but if you play the wrong part of the lane it won't do you any good."

The 12th board, notes Williams, has significance based on your style.
(Photo by Steve Spatafore)

5

PRACTICE

When Mark Baker practices, he does so with a professional's attitude. His seriousness owes to what's at stake.
Baker knows he must work his hardest if he wants to be
that one pro in three who cashes in at the next tournament,
to be one of seven who makes it to match play, or to be the
one out of every forty who gets to the big money of the
televised title round.

What Baker doesn't do is as important as what he
does. He doesn't practice for more than an hour. He doesn't
keep score. And he doesn't feel like being the least bit
sociable until his work is completed.

"When I go to the lanes I have a game plan," Baker
asserts. "I know of players who roll 75 games in a week,
but they don't work on any specific thing. Their idea of
practice is to just throw a lot of shots. That doesn't do you
very much good."

Here's the biggest difference between Baker's concept
and that of the typical bowler. Ask Baker how his practice
went, and he'll analyze how well he fared at honing one
vital part of his game. Put the same question to most folks,

*To score big in games, Baker never keeps score while practicing.
(Photo by Steve Spatafore)*

and the answer will be something like: "It went great. I shot a 219."

Offers Baker, "I very rarely worry about the pins when I'm practicing and I hardly ever keep score." So, too, with Benoit. "If the center has automated scorers, I have them turn them off," says Benoit. "If they have a score-

sheet, I just check off each frame as I bowl. When you keep
score, you lose focus on what it is that you're trying to
practice. I work on specific things, like improving my
release or being as accurate as I can."

There is also the temptation to obtain the best score
possible by following the path of least resistance. If you
roll on your favorite pair of lanes at your favorite center
while using your favorite line with your favorite ball, it's
a good bet that you'll beat your average. But will you have
improved as much as you could have done with a struc-
tured session?

CHALLENGE YOURSELF

Williams knows the characteristics of the various bowling
centers in his hometown of Stockton, California. With rare
exception, he makes it a point "not to play the house shot."
If the best line to the pocket is over the second arrow,
you'll find Williams playing the gutter or deep inside during practice.

He says, "I intentionally use the part of the lane that
has negative area so that my mistakes will be amplified."
Doing so forces him "to make the best possible shot if I am
to strike. I can really tell when I've made an errant shot.
The biggest part of the game is learning how to repeat good
shots."

If he were so inclined, Baker could spend a few hours
rolling strike after strike by using the same ball and by
playing the same line. "That might be good to stroke my
ego," he says, "but it's not going to help me improve or to
keep my competitive edge."

The duration of Baker's sessions ranges from 45 minutes to one hour. "That's the right amount of time for my
needs if I'm really working," he states. "After one hour, my
shirt is soaked with sweat. To me, bowling is not a game,

it's a sport. I work real hard when I'm on the lanes. I don't want anybody talking to me."

Like most veterans in any sport, Williams has long since honed his technique. Yes, there is always some new wrinkle to add to one's arsenal, but his focus is on "staying sharp. I seldom practice for more than an hour and a half."

Part of knowing how to practice is recognizing that more isn't always better. "You can over-practice and burn yourself out," cautions Benoit. "You're not accomplishing a lot when you reach a point at which you're just throwing the ball. If my timing is really bad, I give myself one hour to figure out what's wrong and to make the correction. If I can't do that within an hour, I'll quit for the day.

Benoit's advice: Never practice bad habits by overstaying your welcome. (Photo by Steve Spatafore)

"It's better to walk away than to practice bad habits. If I'm bowling well I might stay for two, three, or four hours. I concentrate on how I feel while making those good shots."

Baker understands the physical keys to his game. He

concentrates on maintaining good timing and on keeping his break point consistent. His typical practice might find him rolling three balls of very different characteristics. After warming up, he'll use each strike ball for about 15 minutes apiece.

Conventional wisdom on the Tour is that an effective practice can only be achieved when you concentrate on one primary objective at a time. Identify the aspect of your delivery that needs work, and then concentrate solely on upgrading it. Offers McDowell, "I try to keep things as simple as possible."

A big part of shooting a 300 is to find the ball that gives you the best chance on that lane condition to strike on shots in which your execution has been less than perfect. But while practicing, McDowell often does the opposite to force himself to make a great shot if he's to get a strike.

> **Identify the aspect of your delivery that needs work, and then concentrate solely on upgrading it.**

McDowell states: "I'll use a hard-shell ball on heavy oil. If I'm able to get a good roll and carry doing that, I will really be able to do some damage in competition with a soft-shell (hooking) ball. Not only does it teach you to roll the ball properly, it also gives you realistic feedback. House conditions tend to be easy. By using the wrong ball, I make them more difficult so that my mistakes are punished. That has made me a much sharper player."

Whereas a golfer or tennis player can work on a wide range of shots, bowling doesn't have as much variety. As such, it's harder to maintain one's concentration for long time periods on the lanes than it is on a court or at a driving range.

Benoit has an unusual way of combating boredom. "I really like music from the 1950s, '60s, and '70s," he relates. "I take my stereo to the lanes. Bowling to music helps me get into a rhythm, remain relaxed, and not have my mind wander."

Williams likes to "practice on as many different conditions as I can." He'll move across the lane, throwing his strike ball from various angles. A typical session might see him using the 5 board, 10 board, 15 board, and 20 board as his targets.

Says Williams: "Once in a while I will keep score to give myself a goal at which to strive. I might play the 20-board shot in a difficult house and hope to bowl 200. After a few days of practicing on really tough conditions, I'll play the house shot just to maintain my confidence that I can produce big numbers."

The tougher the condition on which you practice, the better the quality of shot required to strike. One should take care to avoid bad habits that can come from training exclusively in a so-called graveyard. Offers Baker: "Practicing at a very tough house can be bad if you start forcing your shots as you try to hit the smallest of targets. To bowl well, you have to stay loose."

Continues Baker: "I vary where I practice. A big part of shooting a 300 is how fast you can adjust to the lanes. One reason that the pros shoot so many perfect games is because we face so many different conditions. We're prepared to adjust quickly so we can start striking sooner."

PARTNER UP

Not every session has to be performed in solitude. You might be surprised at the large number of pros who still bowl what are commonly called action matches. Whether the stakes are for big dollars or as minor as having the loser pay for the lanes, the introduction of the competitive aspect adds an important dimension.

"Try to practice with someone who is as good or better than you are," suggests Williams. "Even if it's only for a soda, having that on the line makes me try harder. I try to practice with the best available competition."

Not everyone has a practice partner who is a better bowler. If you wish to simulate match-game pressure, you can always spot your opponent a set number of pins or you can "bet" yourself. Should you reach your target score, treat yourself to something desirable (like an ice cream cone). When you fail to meet your goal, punish yourself. (OK, buddy, give me 50 sit-ups!)

A word to the wise: Only bowl for score after you're satisfied that your game is physically sharp. If it's not, you are better advised to skip the competition and work on the aspect of your delivery that is most in need of attention.

That's why most times you'll find even someone as accomplished as Baker working by himself. If Baker has company, it's a good bet that he's not on top of his game. Baker explains: "When I'm bowling good, I don't want anyone helping me. When I'm struggling, I need to have a coach whom I can trust to work with me. One of the biggest problems in our sport is that we don't have enough good coaching."

For several years, Baker's exclusive personal instructor was Bill Julian. Lately, he's also worked with noted coach John Jowdy and fellow PBA stars David Husted, Jeff Bellinger, and Ricky Corona. In addition to being well-versed in the fundamentals of bowling, an expert knows how to recognize the difference between a well-executed delivery and one that's flawed.

Baker says: "I need for someone who knows what they're doing to be honest with me. Every time that I strike, I haven't necessarily made a good shot. It might just be that the condition is very easy. There are also times when I can't buy a strike when I'm actually bowling fairly well on a difficult condition.

"You have to know whether it's you or the lanes that

Even great players like Johnny Petraglia (left)
need help. Here, Petraglia gets some pointers from
the highly respected coach of many of the pros, John
Jowdy. (Photo by Dan Herbst)

are responsible for a strike or for a miss." Even for a pro,
it's a huge plus to have someone who knows both the sport
and your game to help you escape a slump.

COACHING YOURSELF

The next best thing is to engage in accurate self-analysis.
Through experience, McDowell discovered that he gets in
trouble when his loft is excessive. The greater the distance
that his shot travels before landing on the lane, the more
that McDowell had hit up on his release rather than having
projected the ball out onto the lane (remember our analogy
of the airplane landing on a runway).

McDowell's bar is a practice aid that reminds him to be smooth.
(Photo by Steve Spatafore)

Inspired by an idea from Hall of Fame coach John Jowdy, McDowell devised a practice tool to combat that mistake. He places a one-foot-high crossbar across the lane approximately six feet from the foul line. That forces him to concentrate on rolling the ball smoothly so as not to strike the bar.

Instead of throwing in the towel when the heads break down, learn how to overcome that condition by throwing practice shots over a towel. (Photo by Steve Spatafore)

Conversely, some players set the ball "short." Instead of projecting the ball softly onto the surface, they drop it at the bottom of the backswing. This causes a loss of both power and accuracy. To work on the solution, place an object (like a towel) on the other side of the foul line. Concentrate on getting your ball to land just beyond the object.

Although shooting a 300 means you won't be faced with any 10 pins, the chances are pretty good that not very many games will see you going 12 for 12 in the strike department. Spare shooting remains an essential element in the successful player's bag of tricks. Baker dedicates "5 to 10 shots of every practice to working on my toughest spare."

If you are preparing for a specific event to be contested on a specific condition, find a center to practice where the lanes most closely resemble those on which you'll be competing.

SHAPE UP

To do well on different conditions, it pays to be in condition. More and more contemporary stars attribute their on-lanes feats to off-lanes work. True, the best way to improve your bowling is to bowl (in fancy modern sports terminology it's known as "functional training"). But being fit is also important. It can give you a big edge over the many bowlers who mistakenly assume that just because you don't have to run or jump to throw a stike, being in shape isn't important.

States Baker: "Being in excellent physical condition will definitely give you a great mental edge on 95 percent of the bowlers at all levels of competition. When I got out of shape in the mid-1980s, I had to practice more just to keep that same feel to my game because my knee bend wasn't as strong."

Baker attributes the success of Amleto Monacelli as much to physical conditioning as to the Venezuelan's outstanding release: "The only thing that he has to concentrate on when he's bowling is to strike because he has that peace of mind and confidence that comes from knowing he can outlast everybody else. He knows that he's put in every possible effort to get to where he's at."

Monacelli, like the great Marshall Holman, probably rolls as few practice games as any Touring pro. Both stars believe in practicing only as much as required to remain sharp coupled with being physically fit. Says Baker: "Marshall is thought of as a guy who plays a lot of golf and doesn't spend that much time on the lanes. Believe me, he's in great shape. I've gone mountain biking with him, and he just flies up even the steepest hills."

McDowell agrees: "Being in shape gives me an advantage over the guys who don't train. I've seen too many players gain weight after coming on Tour. We're constantly on the go, and it takes an extra effort to be sure to eat

McDowell's great fitness gives him an edge. (Photo by Steve Spatafore)

right. The guys who constantly eat junk food and don't work out don't tend to be very successful."

That's why 1992 Player of the Year Dave Ferraro built a gym in his home. It's why his closest rival for that honor, McDowell, spends countless hours bicycling, jogging, doing sit-ups, and using training equipment.

Because human bodies aren't colliding on the lanes as they do in football or ice hockey, many people mistakenly believe that bowlers aren't vulnerable to injuries. While we're highly unlikely to suffer from broken bones or torn ligaments, we're hardly immune to being disabled.

Having seen many pros hampered by various ailments, Williams engages in what he labels "a preventive maintenance" program. "Bowlers tend to get a lot of overuse type injuries that are caused by cumulative wear and tear," Williams explains. "Those types are slow to develop, but they take a long time to heal and they can become chronic."

Like most pros, Williams stretches extensively prior to bowling. He warms up his muscles before rolling his first shot. A comprehensive stretching routine should include the forearms, groin, wrists, shoulders, and legs.

While McDowell disdains heavy weightlifting, he understands the importance of strengthening his more

Stretching is an important part of a comprehensive warmup. (Photo by Steve Spatafore)

vulnerable body parts. He finds that wrist curls are an important part of that process.

When Benoit changed his style, it became apparent that he had to become stronger to withstand the tougher demands that he was going to be placing on his body. Recollects Benoit: "I worked out a lot with weights. My goal wasn't to build bulk in my chest or my arms. I wanted to build up my right wrist and forearm. I spent hours on the couch working with a 15-pound dumbbell."

His basic exercise was to place his right forearm on his right thigh. He'd let his wrist bend backward to allow the weight to roll from his palm to his fingertips. Then he'd

roll it back from the fingertips to the palm while cocking
the wrist.

He'd also do it with his palm facing downward while
holding the weight in his hand as his wrist changed positions.

Unlike some pros, Benoit never felt compelled to do a
lot of running or jumping rope. His legs were strengthened
by working in a body shop and playing softball. You'd be
amazed at what lifting and moving heavy bumpers can do
for one's power.

The more torque that you impart per shot, the more
stress that your body must withstand. It's vital if you have
a power-oriented game that you adequately prepare your
body. Not only will that enable you to bowl better, it
should also help prevent injuries.

PAYING THE PRICE

Another factor that separates the greats in any endeavor from the pack is their dedication. While most basketball players are content to spend their summers resting, Magic Johnson labored for endless hours improving his shooting. By turning what had been a relatively weak link in his game into an asset, Johnson became an even greater player.

So, too, with Monacelli and Pete Weber. Not content with the success they enjoyed early in their careers, each dedicated himself to upgrading a specific aspect of his game, according to Baker. "Amleto really worked hard on his spare shooting," Baker says. "Now that he doesn't donate pins, those six-baggers really add up. Pete practiced on toning down his strike ball and on becoming more versatile."

Those two, virtually certain future Hall of Fame members, understand that the difference between being good and being great is a matter of what you do best and of eliminating your weaknesses.

ATTITUDE IS KEY

The bottom line, says Baker, is that "it's not enough just to bowl. You have to really work on your bowling.

"Ours is a game of repetition," he reasons. "The players who throw the most strikes are the players whose deliveries are the most consistent. Whenever I practice, I go to the lanes with a purpose. It's common for a basketball player to stay at practice until making 20 consecutive free throws. I do something similar. I'll tell myself that it's the ninth frame of a big match and that I must strike out to win."

Your attitude is really put to the test when you're suffering through a slump. Expect that several well-mean-ing friends will be offering advice. "If you listen to every-one, you'll probably become totally confused," says Mc-Dowell. "The more that I'm struggling, the more important that I only listen to the advice from the one coach who really knows my game. When you try to do everything that everyone is telling you to do, you just get farther and farther away from your natural game. The next thing that you know, you've gotten deeper and deeper into your slump."

The way to escape a slump or to improve when you're hot is the same. In bowling, as in life, there is no shortcut for hard and purposeful work. Plan your practice carefully, put 100 percent into every delivery that you execute, and only work for as long as you can concentrate on the task at hand.

6

THE 12TH SHOT

In many ways, the 12th shot is similar to giving birth: You treat the delivery like it will be your last, a proper breathing technique provides an essential relaxation device, and after it's all over, the pain is forgotten amidst the euphoria.

Here, we provide our version of the Lamaze Method, bowling-style. With apologies to Fernand Lamaze we will skip the ice chips and cut straight to the chase.

You are under pressure. Your nervousness grows because, unlike the pros, you realize that you aren't likely to get this opportunity again in the foreseeable future. Those background noises have disappeared. All eyes are glaring at you. What to do?

STEP 1: ENJOY THE MOMENT

Remind yourself that pressure is merely the reward that you reap for having performed well. The player with six opens isn't under pressure, nor is the team that trails by 95 pins going into the final frame. Pressure only weighs on those who have performed well enough to have something at stake.

View the next few moments as an enjoyable experience in which you will test yourself. The worst that can happen doesn't involve your health, your family, or even a letter from the IRS in your mailbox.

If you succeed, you will have something to tell the kids. If you fail, you will still have something to tell the kids. Either way, the freeway will remain crowded in the morning, you won't lose your job, taxes won't go down, and one billion folks in China couldn't care less.

In other words, remember that it's only a game.

STEP 2: BE CONFIDENT

At the moment, the person who is bowling better than anyone else in the center, maybe even in the entire state, is you (yes, you). So assume that you can achieve one more time what you have just done 11 shots in a row.

If you spend the moments between frames thinking about the consequences of success or failure, and blowing both out of proportion, you will find it very difficult to achieve the relaxation that's required to make your best shot. A far better bet is to enjoy the moment, perhaps even laughing to yourself about the incongruity. ("Imagine, all these people watching me bowl! That's like paying money to take a spelling class taught by Dan Quayle.")

Bowling should always be fun. What could be more enjoyable than knowing that you have already produced an exceptional score? After all, had someone told you at the start of the night that you would roll a 297, a 298, or a 299, we're sure you would have agreed to take it.

The odds are great that you have already guaranteed yourself of rolling the best game in your league for the season, and you're also well on your way to a shot at a high series. If you look at it from the perspective that you have nothing to lose and everything to gain, your chances of getting that last strike will greatly increase.

In sports, as in life, expectations often dictate reality. McDowell offers that one of the major reasons why the pros usually perform in the 10th frame to complete a perfect game is that they are confident. Making matters easier is that even with a packed center, there probably is less pressure on them than there is on one of us.

Which brings us to the C-word. What of the player among us who chokes on the 12th ball? "Give him credit," reasons Baker, "for having been in a position to choke while the rest of us were watching him perform. You have to bowl great to put yourself in a position to choke."

Besides, this isn't really pressure. Battling cancer is pressure. Flying a mission over enemy lines is pressure. Performing brain surgery is pressure. Bowling, at all but the highest levels, is recreation.

Still, there is nothing wrong with being nervous. Heck, you should be nervous. Anyone who is impervious to the excitement inherent in the situation can't be fully human. Know that you can perform while nervous. Don't allow yourself to become fearful.

One of the most intense moments in tenpin history occurred on January 31, 1987, in Torrance, California. Pete McCordic stood on the approach at Gable House Bowl but one strike removed from becoming the first pro in 13 years to roll a televised 300. So nervous was McCordic that even those in the cheap seats had to notice his quivering.

The camera close-up on ABC-TV gave viewers a rare glimpse at just how much pressure a player can feel. McCordic knew that $100,000 was riding on that last shot. That's a pretty fair chunk of change to anyone, but especially so on the PBA Tour given that the vast majority of players, McCordic included, are pleased to enjoy a net profit of even half that sum in a typical year.

*Pete McCordic
had both 300 (pins)
and 100,000 (dollars)
reasons to smile on
January 31, 1987.
(Photo courtesy
of the PBA)*

McCordic pulled his shot ever so slightly. The 4 pin was the last to fall. McCordic, his arms raised toward the heavens in triumph and relief, had just demonstrated the qualities that separate the best professional bowlers from the pack. Lots of guys can string strikes in practice. The great athlete, in any sport, is able to perform his best when the pressure is the greatest.

Afterward, McCordic acknowledged that he was a bundle of nerves but that experience had taught him that he could bowl well while he was nervous. You can, too. And there's a lot less riding on your shot than there was on McCordic's.

STEP 3:
CONCENTRATE ON THE TASK AT HAND

It's easy to get caught up in the moment. If you are a serious bowler, chances are that you have come to understand your "choke tendency." That phrase refers to the physical flaw that usually results when you fail to make your best shot while under stress.

Some of us "rear up" at the foul line instead of staying down with the shot. If that's you, concentrate on watching your ball until at least after it has rolled past the arrows.

Other players get "fast feet," "tug" their shots, drop the shoulder of the bowling arm, or get "soft" with ball speed. We'll translate these in due time.

Suffice it to say, for now, that you probably know what you are most likely to do wrong in a pressure situation. If not, you haven't been paying enough attention to past performances.

It's important that you analyze key shots after they are over to better understand what you did (or didn't do) right. Let's say you were right of the pocket. Ask yourself: Did I miss my target to the right, drop my shoulder, or throw the ball too hard?

If your ball went through the nose, you need to know if it was because you missed your target to the left or you

Through experience, McDowell has learned the importance of staying down with his shot while performing under pressure. (Photo by Steve Spatafore)

rolled your hook ball at a slower speed (known as being "soft").

You must try to determine if your timing was flawed or, perhaps, your pushaway and armswing were off line. Only when you identify the cause of the mistake can you attempt to implement a correction on shots in subsequent tension-filled moments.

Knowing your own tendencies is very helpful when it comes time to put yourself to the test. That allows you to remind yourself what to do ("just stay down with the shot").

STEP 4: RELAX

One of the most challenging parts of a bowler's task is to be aggressive and relaxed simultaneously. The ability to reconcile that seemingly incompatible mix is one of the qualities that separates great players from the rest.

STEP 5: KEEP IT IN PERSPECTIVE

There are two main reasons why the pros roll so many perfect games. The first factor is their physical abilities. The other half of the equation involves their thought processes. Not only are they knowledgeable about adjustments and confident in their abilities, they also don't blow things out of proportion.

One of the biggest dangers involved in rolling a 300 is the letdown one suffers afterward. A pro simply can't afford a bad score. Maintaining an emotional even keel during good games and poor ones is important.

Except for rolling a televised 300, shooting a perfect game doesn't put a lot of money into a pro's pocket. Pros' attitudes toward the subject are typified by Williams's analysis: "It's more of a spectator thing. A 300 game is nice, but it's only one more pin than a 299 on the scoresheet."

STEP 6: LAST-SHOT STRATEGY

You certainly don't want to wimp out on your 12th ball by being so preoccupied with hitting your target that you don't impart any power. "You can get too careful," Williams notes.

Having said that, however, the far greater danger is getting fast with your feet and your ball speed. Count on your adrenaline to kick in. There are two schools of thought when that occurs. Some players make an adjustment to counteract the effects of the added adrenaline by redoubling their efforts to duplicate their previous series of motions. Others compensate for it by slightly changing the way they play the lane.

Among those opting for the latter is Baker. Through experience, he has discovered that the excitement he feels when going for a 300 is such that he won't deliver his 12th shot in the same manner as he did his first ball.

With his heart beating faster, Baker knows that he will naturally throw his final shot harder. The difference is enough to cut down his hook by a few boards. If his release, aiming point, and position on the approach don't differ, Baker will be frustrated by his failure to carry the resulting light hits.

"My biggest secret," Baker relates, "is that on my last ball I move my feet to the right and my target to the right. Nobody strokes that last shot. You see a lot of 2 pins and 5 pins left because a player's adrenaline is pumping so much that he throws the ball harder. I know my adrenaline will cause me to roll that last shot one or two miles an hour faster. It's like a golfer who is so pumped up because he's leading a tournament that he only needs an 8-iron from 180 yards out."

In contrast, McDowell prefers to live by that grammatically hideous sports cliche that says "you dance with who brung you."

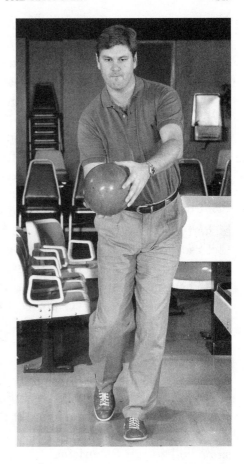

The sixth-leading money winner of 1985 and 1986 compensates in advance for his adrenaline rush when closing in on a 300. (Photo by Steve Spatafore)

Asserts McDowell: "I stay where I am on the lane and I try to play the same shot. By nature I have a fairly compact approach, so there have been occasions in which I have pulled the ball back into my armswing and then pulled it forward. To avoid that, I try to stay loose and relaxed to keep my rhythm going."

One trick is that before his delivery McDowell will allow the ball to swing freely. He likens that to the golfer who "swings" an imaginary club as he walks up the fairway.

The biggest problem many amateurs face, according to

Baker, is that "they try to bowl a 300 in the eighth or ninth frame instead of just hitting the pocket. They break their rhythm instead of just letting it happen. The next thing you know, they have gotten too fast with their feet."

Baker thinks that one reason he's been so much more successful than his peers in the 10th frame is that his normal ball speed is faster than most. Because of that, his key deliveries aren't that different from the rest. What's far tougher, he believes, is for a player with naturally slow speed (like Benoit) to maintain that pace under pressure.

Like Baker, Williams is a good finisher. At last count he had 31 perfect games (27 in PBA play and four others that received ABC sanctioning). By his estimate, he's had the first 11 strikes "about 40 times."

There is no one set formula that he uses. Offers Williams: "Sometimes I try for power. I tend to throw it better when I play more straight. A lot of shooting a 300 involves your confidence."

So what differs on his 12th shot? Nothing, he hopes. "I don't try to do anything differently. To me, it doesn't make any sense to successfully do something for 11 shots only to change it on the 12th. You can out-think yourself."

Is that because, unlike Baker, Williams maintains the same ball speed? Surprisingly, he says not. "I probably do tend to throw it a little harder under pressure. But I stand in the same place and I try to throw it the same."

Because the excitement builds from frame to frame, Williams believes that his ball speed tends to increase in increments as the game progresses. Even though the 12th shot may have more velocity than its immediate predecessor, it won't be that much different.

Benoit cautions against trying to be "too perfect." He acknowledges that his ability to finish a 300 has run the gamut from periods of time when he got the 12th strike nearly every time to other streaks in which he seemingly couldn't buy that final "X."

His longest 300 slump occurred, ironically, just after his Texas title-game windfall. With the benefit of hindsight, he blames the problem on his having tried a bit too hard. "I was trying to prove myself to the fans," he admits. "I felt that after that 300 on TV that spectators felt that I was expected to get that 12th one."

Instead, his final-shot results were less than satisfactory. "I was leaving garbage all over the place," Benoit says.

Benoit has also shot several 300s in a single month. The biggest difference between the periods in which he's successful on the last shot compared to when he isn't involves his mental game.

He knows that a good cycle is coming when his better scores start reaching into the 270s. At that point he be-

Unlike Baker, Williams doesn't change a thing for his critical 12th shot. (Photo by Steve Spatafore)

comes convinced that he's hot. "I tell myself, 'here comes the pattern,'" says Benoit. "I get into a cycle and I feel that a 300 will happen at any moment. I can also handle the bad games better because I'm convinced that I'm in my cycle and that nothing can go wrong."

After his early troubles finishing what he'd started, McDowell has gained a reputation as someone who is more likely than not to claim that final "X." Perhaps, he offers, that's due to his new perspective.

Visualize.
Follow a Pre-Shot Routine.
Think Positive.
Just Do It.

When McDowell was in college, the biggest pressure he felt was to shoot a 300. The title round (with its $100,000 windfall) notwithstanding, rolling a perfect game on Tour represents a nice feat, but it's hardly as important as being able to double in the 10th frame to win a contest in either match play or the championship round.

McDowell felt a lot more pressure during the climactic game of the 1992 Firestone, in which the stakes included a $27,000 pay differential ($60,000 to the winner; $33,000 to the runner-up), assorted manufacturers' bonuses, potential endorsement revenues, as well as a five-year exemption into professional bowling's most prestigious event. The value of that package certainly eclipses the standard Tour reward of $100 and a diamond chip that one gets for shooting a nontelevised perfect game.

Among the "thank-yous" McDowell bestowed following his greatest triumph was one to clinical hypnotherapist Jack Blumenthal. "Frankly," McDowell acknowledged to the media, "I don't think I was capable of winning this tournament a couple of years ago."

The difference came after McDowell gained valuable experience and swapped personalized positive-reinforcement tapes in exchange for bowling lessons for Blumenthal's son. (And you thought the Red Sox selling Babe Ruth to the Yankees for $125,000 was one-sided!)

There are a few devices you can use to ease your mind so that it, in turn, will help relax your body:

1. Visualize. Try to picture yourself rolling a great shot for a strike. That shouldn't be hard to do given that you won't have to think very far back to summon up a positive image.
2. Follow a Pre-Shot Routine. Always repeat the same series of actions prior to stepping onto the approach. There is always some comfort to be found in doing what's familiar.
3. Think Positive. You know you can strike. Heck, you've done nothing but strike all game. Tell yourself, "I've struck thousands of times in my life. I can do it again."
4. Just Do It. We hate to sound like a sneaker commercial, but it is important that you don't significantly alter the amount of time it takes you to begin your delivery. Unless you are a naturally deliberate player, the longer you stand in the address position, the more likely you are to freeze.

STEP 7: THE HARD PART IS OVER

Baker isn't the only member of our team who thinks that the final strike is far easier than was number 10. Benoit concurs: "The first two shots in the 10th frame are harder to get. After the ninth frame, you have to sit there as everyone else bowls. There's a lot of time in which you have to think about it."

One can think too much. When he hasn't been as successful in finishing a 300, Benoit admits that he's "taken too long and tried too hard to be more exact. I've tried to be too perfect. Sometimes you need to just let the ball go."

*While you should always strive to make a good
shot, Benoit cautions against attempting to be
"too perfect." (Photo by Steve Spatafore)*

The more confident Benoit is at the time, the less likely
he is to make a minor adjustment. The less likely he is to
adjust, the more likely he is to shoot that 300.

Continues Benoit: "Let's say your 10th shot is a bit
light and the 11th ball is a little bit high. Should you try
something different on the last ball? I wouldn't.

"Everyone wants to see that perfect pocket hit in
which the pins explode and there's nothing left on the
deck. I'm guilty of that, too. But ugly strikes count just as
much as the pretty ones. Sometimes I catch myself thinking, 'don't get too far right like on the last shot, don't tug it,
and don't get fast with your feet.' Those are all negative

thoughts. How can you create a positive result when you are thinking only about avoiding something negative? I say to forget about the 11th strike and just throw the last shot as best as you can."

STEP 8: RELAXATION TECHNIQUES

What about my breathing? you may ask. All four pros are definitely in favor of it. For one, it supplies oxygen to the brain and, rumor has it, failure to breathe isn't particularly good for your health.

Research has also shown that a deep breath definitely relaxes one's muscles. After you pick the ball out of the rack, treat yourself to a giant-size inhale. Remind yourself of your number one physical key. You are now ready to roll.

When you review this chapter (yes, class, we hope that you may be "road tested" on it someday), you will notice that our pros aren't unanimous on 12th-shot strategy. Just as there is no one way to skin the proverbial cat, there are many different valid ideas about what to do on your climactic delivery.

If there is one thing upon which our team agrees, it's to remain calm and to enjoy your moment in the sun. Paul Simon once sang that one man's ceiling is another man's floor. What might be debilitating pressure to some is fun to others. When asked why he remains one of bowling's finest pressure performers, all-time great Dick Weber often laughs and concedes, "I'm a ham."

That may not sound like a very scientific explanation, but it's as accurate as any. As with Weber, the only man to have captured a PBA title in five different decades, the biggest key that's common to us all is to simply enjoy the moment. It would be a shame if you looked back on the best game that you ever rolled and realized that you didn't have fun at the time.

7

MAINTAINING A POSITIVE ATTITUDE

"You would be amazed," observes McDowell, "at how many professional bowlers have the physical talent to do well but whose attitude doesn't allow them to be successful."

Like many of his peers, McDowell says that consulting a sports psychologist has greatly improved his performance, especially in pressure situations. It's not enough to have a good armswing, timing, and release. To bag that 300 requires that you be able to deal with a potentially stressful circumstance in a positive manner.

Picture the situation that you will find yourself facing. As the strikes mount, more and more of your fellow bowlers have noticed your score. As you step onto the approach with each passing frame, the center becomes less noisy, more people are watching, and players on adjacent lanes are making a point to yield the right of way. You perceive a difference in the way that your teammates and opponents are communicating with you between shots.

By the 10th frame, the atmosphere has changed as dramatically as British weather. Dozens of people are

standing behind your pair of lanes, many straining on their
tiptoes to glimpse your next shot. A discomforting quiet
prevails. The pressure is definitely on.

"When I'm in that situation, I smile to myself," Baker
says. "Every pro athlete has some ham in him, and I'm no
exception. I remind myself that it's for such moments that
I bowl. Tell yourself, 'This is why I've practiced so hard.
This is why I bought that new ball. This is why I read that
instructional book.'

Baker reminds you to enjoy the limelight.
(Photo by Steve Spatafore)

"You should know that every other bowler there wishes they were in your shoes. If you shoot a 300, you'll have a blast. If not, you'll shoot a 270, which is still a great game."

According to Williams, the two key components of the mental game are good concentration coupled with a positive attitude. Achieving those qualities comes under the heading of easier said than done.

Baker, Williams, and McDowell all credit experiences in another sport with helping them focus on the task at hand. Baker knows what it's like to stand at the free throw line in a critical situation while opposing fans are doing everything in their power to unnerve the shooter. As a collegian, McDowell booted field goals and played a lot of darts. Achieving success at either of those, he says, is as much mental as physical. In competitive horseshoes, Williams notes, spectators are always moving around behind

Williams says horseshoes helps his tenpin game. (Photo by Steve Spatafore)

the stake. "I've learned not to let that bother me," he states.

Contrast their perspective with that of some bowlers you know who become visibly angry at the smallest of distractions. Who among us has not seen someone slam a ball back onto the rack after being cut off by a player on the next lane or when some unexpected noise (such as a ringing phone or the foul-light buzzer) bothers him or her during the delivery?

Anger, according to experts in sports behavior, is counterproductive. That's especially true in bowling. Even in as physically taxing an activity as boxing or football in which one can "punish" an opponent, loss of composure must be avoided. The quicker your temper, the slower your successes will come.

To bowl well, you need a calm head to analyze your shots and to produce a relaxed delivery. The adrenaline rush and increased heart rate that accompany a surge of annoyance make it far more difficult to produce a good shot.

Of course, there are "stars" who aren't exactly known for maintaining an even keel. To some, their success disproves our sentiments that anger hinders performance. To us, a closer analysis of the effects of their temper seems to indicate that they would have been far more successful with a calmer nature.

Perhaps the best example is that of Marshall Holman. Without a doubt he is one of the greatest players in bowling history. Holman is very intelligent, in great condition, and his physical skills are the envy of virtually all of his fellow pros.

Despite his having won 21 PBA titles (as of press time), many pros will concede "off the record" that he is their favorite opponent to face in a championship round. At the first sign of bad luck, he's been known to unravel.

Most great players exude an aura of confidence that can unnerve a less-experienced opponent. In contrast, because Holman has been known to beat himself at the slightest provocation, those facing him are more at ease.

In a diplomatic manner, McDowell is willing to articulate what virtually all of his peers think. Asserts McDowell: "Marshall could have won more titles if he'd kept his emotions more under control. Players with bad tempers tend to beat themselves."

McDowell should know. Although he was never among the Tour's hotheads, he freely admits that he wasn't always as mature as he is today. "I had my share of angry moments while bowling," he concedes. "As I look back, I can't think of a single instance in which getting mad helped me to bowl better. I'm still an emotional player. That's just my personality. The difference is that now I'm careful to keep my emotions within acceptable limits."

WHY YOU SHOULD NEVER QUIT

It's amazing how many 300s are rolled by players who are coming off a mediocre game. If you become disgusted when things aren't going your way, you stand very little chance of turning things around that night. "If you never give up," McDowell notes, "good things can still happen. A lot of bowlers throw in the towel before they should. So many guys don't realize how close they are to being successful when they give up."

That lack of maturity can prove one's undoing. Consider the case of a 1992 Bowler of the Year candidate who was among the leaders of a big tournament on the PBA fall Tour with but a few games of match play remaining. As can happen to anyone, he suffered a poor game that dropped him in the standings but still left him with an outside chance of qualifying for the title round.

McDowell picks up the tale: "Instead of redoubling his effort to turn it around and shoot two big games, which he was capable of doing, he became totally frustrated. Maybe he didn't realize how close he still was to making the (TV) show. He didn't even seem to care how he did the last two games."

Our subject dropped to an 11th-place finish. There is no telling how much better he would have fared if he had Williams's attitude. Says Williams: "Until you're mathematically eliminated, you've got to try on every shot. Even if it takes 36 strikes in a row, tell yourself it can be done."

Hall of Fame member Mike Durbin has a philosophy that is worth remembering. Durbin is fond of saying that "if it can be done with a pencil, it can be done with a bowling ball."

Even when a game (or tournament) can't be won, it behooves you to keep trying. "In that situation I will tell myself to practice," relates Williams. "To be sure, it's an expensive form of practice. There is always something that you can work on to improve your game."

McDowell "continually sets goals" for himself. "If I'm 16th with a few games remaining and I know that I can't make the title round, I will try to finish in the top 10," McDowell says.

There are times in league play in which it's clear that the outcome of that game and of total wood has been decided. At that point you can go through the motions or you can fully concentrate.

Let's say that you have trouble striking while playing a deep inside line. Why not try that line for a few frames? Or, better still, why not experiment with a different ball or line in an effort to discover a better formula for the next time out?

As long as you continue to work hard, you give yourself a chance to improve and you maintain the sense of self-satisfaction that comes from perseverance.

Williams says that having a good sense of humor and

Nobody in the history of the PBA has ever pro-
duced more perfect games in a tournament on the
national circuit than 1986's Player of the Year.
(Photo by Steve Spatafore)

keeping things in perspective helps. He tells the story of a
fellow pro who, following a bad outing, retired to the
lounge to complain bitterly about the lane conditions, the
host bowling center, and anything else that came to his

mind. His tirade ended abruptly when he discovered that the gentleman at the next table had recently been released after having been a hostage in Iran.

Baker observes: "We all start out in this game because we enjoy it. It's a shame that when many people become good at it that they stop having as much fun. A lot of amateurs are more intense than I am. Even for those of us who bowl for a living, it's important to have fun. One reason I've done so well is that I like being out there, even when I'm having a bad day. If bowling isn't fun for you, something's wrong. Don't make it a life and death issue."

GOING FOR THE 300

If the best moment of your bowling career isn't fun, something is very wrong. Ironically, says Baker, the biggest key to completing that 300 is "not trying to strike."

Continues Baker: "Instead of just trying to throw a good shot, most people try to strike. As a result, they rear up at the line because they're overanxious to see their shot. You've got to stay down at the line and, like golf, keep your head down. I don't look up until after my ball has rolled over the target."

One thing to keep in mind is that everything you've done so far in that game has worked. There is no need to try to make a better shot. You also know that you're enjoying a perfect carry percentage. Cautions Baker: "Invariably I bowl poorly when the lanes are easy and I try to strike. I'll be all right if I can just make good shots and hit the pocket."

A very difficult aspect of shooting a 300 is handling the down time between frames. What usually happens when a basketball player needs to make two free throws in a critical spot or a placekicker is faced with a field goal attempt with a game on the line? More times than not the opposing coach calls a timeout to freeze the player on the spot. There's a sports adage that says "think long, think wrong."

The bowler chasing a perfect game must always perform after enduring a considerable between-shot wait. If Baker appears calm at such times, it's because he's not thinking about what's at stake.

Says Baker: "I think of something relaxing like being on a sailboat enjoying the gentle sway of the ocean. It's been proven that comforting thoughts decrease the heart rate. Not until I step onto the approach do my thoughts return to making a good shot."

Benoit, like many pros, likes to "listen" to a favorite tune that goes through his mind. He's big on oldies such as "Unchained Melody," "This Magic Moment," and "Hey There, Lonely Girl." Such mellow tunes help maintain a more relaxed state.

Adds McDowell: "You can't think about how much the next few shots mean or the pressure that's involved. If you let thoughts like that come into your head, you'll be in trouble. You have to shut out those distractions to stay relaxed and to concentrate on executing a good delivery. At times like that, I block everything else out of my mind. I'm in my own little world concentrating on the task that I must perform."

Many pros find it far easier to complete a perfect game than they do to strike out to win a title. That's because the latter is far more lucrative to them than is rolling another 300. Even with their ability to deal with stress, they fare better when less is at stake because they remain more relaxed.

There are exceptions. The truly great players do better when more is on the line. You don't want to be sitting on the bench at the end of your game when Pete Weber, Mike Aulby, or Del Ballard, Jr., needs a double to beat you.

To make his mark in the clutch, McDowell strives for a state of controlled intensity. (Photo by Steve Spatafore)

McDowell describes their attitude as one of "controlled intensity. That's not an easy state to achieve. Pete is incredibly intense, yet he's under control. When he has a chance to win, Aulby is like a shark with blood in the area."

Another key part of the equation is convincing yourself that you will make a good shot when under pressure. For many years, McDowell didn't fare well as the top seed of the stepladder format title round on television. He tried to a analyze what qualities Weber and Parker Bohn III possessed that allowed them to thrive when in the same situation. McDowell's conclusion: "They have supreme confidence in themselves. They *know* that they're going to win."

Contrast that with McDowell's attitude early in his pro career. "I was *hoping* to win," he recalls.

McDowell appeared in seven title rounds in 1991 and again in 1992. He failed to capture a tournament that first year but made three trips to the winner's circle the following season. He credits part of the difference to having worked with clinical hypnotherapist Jack Blumenthal. After several discussions, it became apparent that McDowell lacked the level of confidence bordering on arrogance that helps the great players excel.

"Even though I had defeated the best players from time to time, I always felt that I wasn't quite on par with them," McDowell admits. "I had put Holman, Monacelli, Weber, and Ballard on a pedestal. I needed to believe that I belonged in their category. Now I do."

Some players use visualization techniques. Picture yourself executing the perfect delivery. That's equally helpful when you're doing well (to reinforce your confidence) as it is to get you out of a rut. In the latter situation, McDowell sometimes thinks of the picture-perfect style of Brian Voss. States McDowell, "I envision how he flows to the line, and I try to imitate that."

Baker adds, "If you see yourself doing it right over and over, it becomes easier to translate those movements to the physical. To see yourself using your best form to hit your target and the pocket gives you a good feeling inside.

"Anything that you do to reinforce positive thoughts is good. If you think that you're going to throw a strike, you increase your chances of striking. If you think to yourself, 'don't choke,' you're done."

HANDLING THE RESULTS

Sometimes you throw a seemingly great shot and get robbed. Other times a poor effort results in a strike. If the former deprives you of that perfect game, you're bound to think: Is there no justice in bowling?

At times, there isn't. But the only thing that falls when you curse or kick the ball return is people's opinion of you, not the pins. You did your best, and you gave it a great shot. That, alone, ought to bring a smile to your face. You should gain confidence by knowing

Anything that you do to reinforce positive thoughts is good.

that you made a good shot under pressure, which certainly bodes well for your chances at getting that perfect game the next time that you're in contention for one.

Offers McDowell: "I always try to keep myself on an emotional even keel. I realize that some good things are going to happen to me over time and that some bad things will happen. You have to take the good breaks with the bad breaks and accept them both. I learned the value of that by observing Dave Husted and Monacelli. Not getting too excited one way or the other is in your best interest."

Of course, Husted's approach is what works best for him. He's not even an extreme case. Veteran right-hander Dave Arnold is the athletic equivalent of elevator music.

Conversely, Pete Weber is on top of his game when he's most intense. When there's something significant on the line, Weber's eyes are fiery. If pins could be intimidated into falling, there's no doubt that his demeanor would do the trick.

The key is that athletes must be true to their nature. Arnold couldn't perform if he was as fired up as Weber gets. And Weber's game would suffer if he tried to stay as low-key as is Arnold. While it's fine to be intense like Weber, do not mistake anger for intensity. Getting mad only causes a loss in composure, which makes it doubly difficult for you to perform well on subsequent shots.

Even if you look back at a pressure situation in which you didn't execute as you might have wished, chalk it up to a learning experience. Figure out what you can do better the next time, and be thankful for doing well enough to be in a position to perform with something at stake.

Far too many people think that they choked under pressure. It's a term that Baker hates: "You can only choke if you're in a position to choke. Not even the greatest players in the game come through every time."

Agrees Williams: "Sometimes I don't handle the pressure too well and sometimes I do. You have to have a positive self-image. Remember that nobody strikes every time. I try not to see it as an all-important shot. Just remind yourself to throw the ball the same way as you did in the first frame and to do the best that you can."

Regardless of whether it's the first shot or the last, the physical movements that you must execute to strike are the same. The only thing that makes the 10th frame more difficult is that some players tell themselves that it's harder.

As kids, almost all of us walked across a fallen tree over a shallow stream. If we fell, our ankles got damp. The actual act of keeping our balance proved a fairly easy proposition.

But what would happen if that same tree were 50 feet above some rapids? How many of us would dare to try to cross it? The actual physical skills required are no different than before, but the vastly more serious consequence of a failure is why tightrope walkers are one in a million. There are many who have the requisite balance to perform their job but precious few who have the mental proclivity to try.

Understanding that principle is important, for it reminds us that the human mind can be used to work either for our betterment or to our detriment. That's why the difference between achieving that 300 or falling short is often decided by thoughts. You have already demonstrated that you have the physical ability to throw strikes. Now, to complete the perfect game, you must force your mind to think in such a manner as to help your body to perform.

A good tip as you step onto the approach is to ignore the stakes and concentrate on what you must do to make a good shot. States Williams: "One of my keys is to have a good follow-through. I focus on that."

What he has learned not to think about is the fear of failure. "That fear is part of being a human being," he acknowledges. "Nobody wants to fail or to be thought of as a failure."

Even if you get a six count on the last ball for a 296, you haven't failed. Instead, you've succeeded in producing a score that's in the top one-tenth of 1 percent of bowling's highest percentile.

Part of becoming a PBA Touring Pro is having to attend the PBA School. Among the topics covered is the value of positive thinking. At a session that this author observed, the lecturer told the story of Thomas Edison, who, he said, fell short with the first hundred or so formulas for inventing the light bulb. When asked if he had failed, Edison is said to have replied that he had succeeded in discovering 100 ways that one can't make a light bulb!

That sort of perspective is essential if one is to achieve greatness. Benoit is among those who have discovered the power of positive thinking: "I get up, take a deep breath, and just throw it. My goal is just to get my shot over my target. I know that if I hit my arrow at the right speed and angle that my ball is going to hit the 1-3 pocket. Since I'm just concerned with hitting a target rather than striking, I stay a lot looser."

The most lucrative game in the history of the PBA Tour was "meant to be" Benoit's. His recollections of his thought process before and during the contest provide valuable insight.

BENOIT'S RECIPE FOR PERFECTION

As he prepared himself to compete in the championship round of the Quaker State Open, rolling a perfect game was the farthest thing from Benoit's mind. His objective was to claim his first PBA title and, with it, a berth in the Firestone Tournament of Champions.

Benoit knew that some powerful opposition awaited. As the top seed, he would have to face the survivor of a gifted quartet of experienced pros: Mark Roth, Joe Berardi, Brian Voss, or Steve Wunderlich. Roth and Berardi are already in the PBA Hall of Fame, and Voss stands a great chance of joining them.

Benoit's memorable TV debut was against no less a star than 33-time champion Mark Roth. (Photo courtesy of PBA/Steve Spatafore)

"They were all veterans who had been on television," notes Benoit. "I had beaten all four of them during match play so I kept telling myself, 'if you can do it once, you can do it again.' I had a feeling that I'd probably have to face Mark."

The two had squared off in the position-round game the previous evening. Benoit's lead was so substantial entering that game that only a complete unraveling could prevent him from claiming the top berth.

"I had to double in the 10th frame to win that game," states Benoit. Although winning the match had no effect on the standings, Benoit played a mind game with himself. "I pretended that it wasn't the position round but that we were bowling for the title. I wanted to see how I would handle the pressure. Although I knew that the pressure wasn't the same, I wanted to test myself."

This was one exam on which the student got an "A+." Benoit got his double and followed that with a nine count to win that game.

As Saturday's events unfolded, Roth edged Berardi, 223-212, for the right to challenge Benoit. "The biggest thing that I did was not to worry about him at all," says Benoit. "I only worried about what I had to do. Bowling isn't like a fistfight. No matter how intimidating an opponent might seem, there's no physical contact and there's no defense. No matter who you're playing, it's just you against the pins."

When it was Roth's turn to bowl, Benoit visualized his own shot going down the lane before breaking at the ideal spot and hooking into the pocket. Not once did he watch Roth throw a shot.

Having reinforced his confidence with a great warm-up in which he made scores of outstanding shots, Benoit picked up the title game where his practice had left off. Although he remained in a state of deep concentration, he wasn't oblivious as to what was unfolding.

"During the first five or six frames, the applause was fairly noisy after every strike," he recalls. "Around the eighth frame, the cheering became much more intense. The fans were starting to mumble to themselves. I saw (PBA Public Relations Director) Kevin Shippy walk over to get that oversized $100,000 check just in case I struck out.

"Everything seemed to be speeding up. I remembered some advice from (noted bowling coach) Fred Borden. He told me that when adrenaline starts pumping to take a deep breath and to let it out very slowly. That helps to relax the body. I took several deep, slow breaths and then I'd close my eyes to picture myself throwing the next shot."

The most pressure-packed ball was strike number nine. Benoit knew that he was only one good delivery removed from realizing his lifelong goal of capturing a PBA title. After having accomplished that, he had to regain his composure in time for the final frame.

"Once I knew that I'd won, my adrenaline was even greater. The hardest thing was to regain my focus, my rhythm, and to slow down my heart rate. I now had another goal, which was to continue to do what I'd been doing."

When he's in such situations, Benoit avoids glancing at the scoreboard. He gets into his own little world in which he's virtually oblivious to things occurring around him. His attitude: "It's like I will just keep striking and hope that somebody will please tap me on the shoulder after I've thrown the 12th ball so I won't get up to roll a 13th shot! There have been times that I'm so focused on what I'm doing that I've actually sat down after throwing the first strike in the tenth and had to have someone tell me what frame it was."

Like all good players, Benoit doesn't get excited until after he's thrown the decisive shot. He knows that the acts of running, jumping, or letting out a yell all increase one's heart beat. Keeping that emotional even keel is important. Besides, if you do come through, there will be plenty of time to celebrate later.

There is, Benoit reasons, nothing to lose. After all, "why get nervous, because you never have anything until it's actually given to you. It's not like something valuable will be taken away if you don't strike. I keep things simple, think positive thoughts, stay relaxed, and focus on my goal of hitting my target. Only after the ball leaves my hand on that last shot will I start to worry. If it's meant to be, it will be."

Glossary

Arrows: Series of seven triangular designs 14½–15½ feet past the foul line that are placed every fifth board across the lane to serve as aiming points for shots.

Area: The amount of boards (space) that one can miss to either side of one's target and still have the shot hit the pocket.

Axis weight: Method of ball drilling that decreases hook and produces a rollout effect. Usually used only for ultra-power players. The ball's holes are drilled several inches to the left of the label for a right-handed player (right of the label for a left-handed player) with an extra hole placed in the center of the top weight.

Back end: Portion of the lane between the arrows and the pin deck, which consists of softer wood (pine).

Back pitch: Angling of thumbhole backward so the tip of the thumb is extended away from the palm. It is used to help the thumb exit the ball sooner to maximize lift. By far the most common of the various thumb pitches.

Ball sanding: *See* Sanding.

Ball shining: *See* Shining.

Ball track: Portion of the ball that comes in contact with the lane as it rolls down the alley. (*See* Spinner, Semi-roller, and Full roller.)

Bellying: *See* Deep inside line.

Blocked lane: A high-scoring condition whereby the boards closest to the gutters have very little lane conditioner and there is a heavy oil buildup on the center boards, which helps to keep shots in the pocket. If too flagrant it is illegal.

Boards: Strips of wood that extend from the start of the approach to the pins. They are used as both a starting and an aiming point by players. There are 39 boards on a lane.

Breakpoint: The distance from the foul line at which the ball's trajectory reaches the lowest-numbered board during its route to the pocket.

Carrydown: Movement of lane conditioner caused by a succession of shots from beyond where the oil was applied toward the pins. It decreases the ball's hooking on the back end.

Cheater: Slang term for the highly reactive resin-based urethane bowling balls.

Conditioner: *See* Oil.

Conventional grip: Placing one's fingers into the ball up to the second joint. It promotes accuracy but retards lift and striking power. Used primarily by beginning and less advanced players.

Cranker: Bowler who relies more on a big hook and great carrying power than on accuracy to succeed.

Creep speed: A ball that is rolled very slowly.

Deep inside line: A strike line that's popular among big hook players in which the bowler stands on a high-numbered board and aims for a lower-numbered board.

Dots: Series of seven spots found seven feet past the foul line, on the foul line, and also at the two most common starting points on the approach. Each dot is on the same board as a corresponding arrow. Their primary function is to provide a reference point for foot placement. They can also be used for aiming points.

Early timing: Releasing the shot prior to the sliding foot reaching the foul line.

Fifth arrow: The third from the left (for a right-handed player) or from the right (when defined by a left-handed player) of the seven targets painted on the lane. Located on the 25th board.

Finger grips: Inserts placed into finger holes of the ball to promote later release for added lift.

Fingertip grip: Grip whereby the bowler inserts fingers only up to the first joint. Used to promote hook and striking power at the expense of some accuracy.

Finger weight: Drilling of the ball in such a manner that the finger holes are closer to the ball's label than is the thumbhole. It is a form of positive weight. Legal limit is one ounce.

First arrow: The farthest to the right (for a right-handed player) or from the left (when defined by a left-handed player) of the seven targets painted on the lane. Located on the fifth board.

Flip: The curvature of the ball on the back end of the lane.

Forward pitch: Angling of thumbhole inward and/or finger holes upward so the tip of the bowler's thumb is pointing toward the palm and/or the fingers are angled away from the palm. Used for players with small hands and/or short spans to help them grip the ball.

Fourth arrow: The target in the middle of the seven targets painted on the lane. Located on the 20th board.

Front end: The first 18 feet of the lane (also known as "the heads" and the "head area"). On wooden lanes, it consists of maple, a hardwood that is best suited to withstand the wear and tear caused by bowling balls being projected onto it. (The remainder of a wooden lane is made of pine.)

Full roller: Method of rolling a ball in which the track area cuts between the thumb and finger holes. While it once was the shot most frequently used, it is rare among better players today because it lacks the carrying power of the more popular semiroller.

Heads: Front portion of the lane between the foul line and the arrows, which consists of hard wood (maple).

Hit up: A physical error in which the ball is excessively lofted upward during the release in an attempt to produce more revolutions on the shot. In essence, it's an over-exaggerated lift.

Hold area: Amount of margin for error that is provided by an oil buildup in the center of the lane.

Hooking lanes: Dry or lightly oiled condition, which causes maximum hook.

In time: Simultaneous arrival at the foul line of one's sliding foot and release of the ball.

Kickbacks: Hard walls on both sides of the pin deck used to promote pin deflection so pins ricochet back into play. Also known as *sidewalls*.

Kill shot: Shot in which the bowler intentionally reduces the amount the ball will hook.

Lane conditioner: *See* Oil.

Lateral pitch: Angling of thumbhole and/or finger holes to the left or to the right. Thumb pitch affects exit timing. Angling hole to the left for a right-handed player (or to the right for a left-handed bowler) delays thumb release from the ball, while angling to the opposite direction promotes earlier thumb exit. Improper lateral pitch can cause soreness of the thumb.

Late timing: So-called plant-and-shoot method whereby a player releases the shot after the sliding foot has come to a halt.

Leverage weight: Method of drilling the ball so that the holes are a few inches to the left of the label for a right-handed player (or to the right of the label for a left-handed bowler). Its effect is to make the ball skid longer and finish stronger. An extra hole is drilled in the opposite side of the ball. The center of the ball's weight block is thus located between the grip and the balance (extra) hole. The fourth hole is required to keep the weight differential within the legal limit of one ounce.

Leverage window: Zone in which a shot can be released to gain the greatest assistance from the leg muscles for increased carrying power.

Lift: Power imparted to the ball's roll by the thumb exiting the ball first, followed by fingers, hitting through the shot on its release.

Limited distance dressing (LDD): *See* Short oil.

Loading and unloading: *See* Wristing.

Loft: Distance the ball carries after it is released before it hits the lane. When properly executed the shot travels forward, *not* upward or downward.

Lofting: To loft one's shot.

Long oil: Condition in which oil is applied from the foul line to 35 or more feet of the 60-foot lane. Used primarily for PBA and other highly competitive tournaments to create a challenging condition for the advanced-level player.

Lustre King: Machine that applies wax to the surface of bowling balls to prolong ball life and decrease hook.

Maple: Hard wood used for that portion of the lane between the foul line and the arrows.

Negative weight: Use of one or more drilling methods that decrease the ball's amount of hook and/or gets the ball to end its skid and begin its roll pattern sooner. Primarily employed to combat short oil and/or lightly oiled lanes.

Oil: Conditioner applied to a lane's surface that extends life of the alley while retarding ball hook.

Open up a lane: The ability of a power player to create extra area.

Out of bounds: Segment of a lane nearest the gutter on certain oil patterns in which an errant shot will be unable to reach the pocket.

Pin: Where the weight block is located on the inside of the ball.

Pin deck: Portion of the lane housing the pins.

Pin in: Ball construction in which the pin is within an inch of the static center so that the ball will conclude its skid and begin its roll sooner with less back-end flip. It can be extremely effective on a heavily oiled lane.

Pin out: Ball construction in which the pin is two to four inches from the static center. This causes shots to skid farther down the lane with a greater amount of back-end flip. It can be extremely effective on dry lanes.

Pine: Softer wood used for that portion of the lane between the arrows and the pin deck.

Pitch: Angle at which the holes are drilled.

Play the gutter: Strike shot angle in which the ball rolls just inside the gutter before it begins its hooking pattern into the pocket.

Polyester: Substance used for bowling balls that was very popular among pros in the 1970s and remains commonly used by amateur players. Its effect is a cross between urethane and rubber. A polyester ball goes straighter and doesn't hit as well as a urethane ball but hooks more and hits harder than a rubber one. Preferred by advanced-level bowlers where the lanes are exceedingly dry.

Polyurethane: *See* Urethane.

Positive weight: Use of one or more drilling methods that increase the ball's amount of hook and/or get it to conclude its skid and begin its roll pattern late. It is primarily employed to combat long oil and/or heavily oiled lanes.

Power player: *See* Cranker.

Reverse block: Extremely difficult lane condition in which the boards nearest the gutters are heavily oiled while the lane's center is relatively dry.

Reverse pitch: *See* Back pitch.

Revolutions: The number of times the bowling ball rolls over its circumference from when it is released until it reaches the pins. The greater the number, the more striking power usually results. Higher-quality amateur players and strokers usually achieve 10–20 revolutions. The PBA Tour's ultra-power players are usually in the 15–20 range on their strike shots.

Revs: *See* Revolutions.

Ringing 7-pin: Tap suffered by a left-handed player when the 4 pin flies around the 7 pin.

Ringing 10-pin: Tap suffered by a right-handed player when the 6 pin flies around the 10 pin.

Rocket speed: A ball that is rolled very fast.

Rollout: Malady in which the ball uses up most of its impetus early on so little carrying power remains by the time it reaches the pins. The shot will actually stop its hooking pattern as it approaches the pins.

Rubber: Bowling ball surface that remains the most common among house balls. Rubber bowling balls were the balls of choice well into the 1970s until polyester balls were introduced. Rubber balls go straightest and may be useful for covering non-double-wood spares when decreasing hook is necessary on a very dry lane. Very rarely used by advanced players.

Sanding: Using an abrasive substance against the entire surface of the ball. The effect is to get the ball to hook more.

Second arrow: The second from the right (for a right-handed player) or from the left (when defined by a left-handed player) of the seven targets painted on the lane. Located on the 10th board.

Semifingertip grip: Grip in which player inserts fingers into the ball halfway between the first and second joints.

Semiroller: Most popular shot among better-quality players in which the ball's track area can be found just outside of the thumb and finger holes.

Seventh arrow: The farthest to the left (for a right-handed player) or to the right (when defined by a left-handed player) of the seven targets painted on the lane. Located on the 35th board.

Shining: Adding wax to a ball's surface to make it smoother. Used to retard hook and/or extend ball life.

Short oil: Also known as *limited distance dressing* (or *LDD*). Condition in which oil is applied to the front 24 feet (or less) of the lane, thus leaving the final 36 feet (or more) dry.

Shur-Hook: Cork substance used in thumbhole to promote better grip. Commonly used by the player who wants to maintain a similar feel when switching bowling balls.

Sidewalls: Walls to either side of the pin deck off which the pins can ricochet back into play. Also known as *kickbacks.*

Sixth arrow: The second from the left (for a right-handed player) or from the right (when defined by a left-handed player) of the seven targets painted on the lane. Located on the 30th board.

Soft 7-pin: Shot by a left-handed player on which the 7 pin remains as the 4 pin falls weakly into the gutter. Caused by the ball deflecting to the left after colliding with the headpin.

Soft 10-pin: Shot by a right-handed player on which the

10 pin remains as the 6 pin falls weakly into the gutter. Caused by the ball deflecting to the right after it collides with the headpin.

Solid 7-pin: *See* Ringing 7-pin.

Solid 10-pin: *See* Ringing 10-pin.

Spinner: Method of delivering a shot so that only a small portion of the ball (around the 7 o'clock position for right-handers and 5 o'clock for lefties) is in contact with the lane. As a rule this is not a very successful shot for maximizing carrying power and thus is rarely employed by the better-quality bowler.

Straight player: Bowler who places a premium on accuracy at the expense of power.

Stroker: *See* Tweener.

Suitcase grip: Holding the ball like the handle of a suitcase to reduce the amount it will hook.

Swing area: Amount of margin for error to the right of a right-handed player's target (or to the left of a left-handed player's target) that is provided by a lack of conditioner on the lowest numbered boards.

Tap: A single-pin leave on a shot that could have carried.

Third arrow: The third from the right (for a right-handed player) or from the left (when defined by a left-handed player) of the seven targets painted on the lane. Located on the 15th board.

Three-quarter roller: *See* Semiroller.

Thumb grips: Inserts placed inside thumbhole to help player get a better grip. Used primarily to maintain the same feel when player switches bowling balls.

Thumb weight: Method of drilling ball so the thumbhole is closer to the label than are the finger holes. It is a form of negative weight that causes the ball to roll sooner. Maximum legal limit is one ounce.

Tight lanes: Heavy and/or long oil pattern that retards a shot's hook.

Timing: Relationship between the sliding foot and the hand that releases the shot. (*See* Early timing *and* Late timing.)

Top weight: Drilling of ball so that there is up to the maximum legally allowed limit of three ounces more of weight above the label than there is below it. Effect on shot is similar to positive weight.

Track: *See* Ball track.

Track area: Most-used path on the lane to the pocket or the well-worn circle on the ball where it makes contact with the lane.

Tweener: Player who has more accuracy but less power than a cranker and less accuracy but more power than a straight shooter.

Twister: *See* Cranker.

Urethane: Surface substance introduced in bowling balls in early 1980s. Considered state-of-the-art equipment that is noted for its superior gripping of the lane coupled with maximum carrying power.

Walled lane: *See* Blocked lane.

Walls: *See* Kickbacks.

Washout: Spare leave involving the headpin (and possibly other pins to its left) in combination with the 10 pin (for right-handed players) or the headpin (and possibly other pins to its right) in combination with the 7 pin (for left-handed players). Not considered a split.

Weight block: Added section of weight on the inside of the ball. Can be used to maximum advantage by skilled ball driller when placed off center. (*See* Axis weight, Back pitch, Finger weight, Forward pitch, Lateral pitch, Leverage weight, Negative weight, Positive weight, Thumb weight, *and* Top weight.)

Wristing: Method of increasing carrying power by altering the angle of the wrist from a cupped to a flat position during a shot's release.

INDEX